TRAINING ALCOHOL EDUCATORS

A combined training and research perspective

Edited by
Robin Means Lyn Harrison

Occasional Paper 30

UNIVERSITY·OF·BRISTOL
SCHOOL·FOR·ADVANCED·URBAN·STUDIES

The School for Advanced Urban Studies was established jointly by the University of Bristol and the Department of the Environment in 1973 as a post-experience teaching and research centre in the field of urban policy. In addition to the dissemination of material in courses and seminars the School has established three publications series: **SAUS Studies, Occasional Papers and Working Papers.**

SAUS is open to the submission of manuscripts from outside authors within its areas of interest.

General enquiries about the School, its courses, research programme and publications may be addressed to the Publicity Secretary.

School for Advanced Urban Studies
Rodney Lodge
Grange Road
Clifton
Bristol BS8 4EA

Telephone: (0272) 741117

Director: Professor Murray Stewart

SAUS is working to counter discrimination on grounds of gender, race, disability, age and sexuality in all its activities.

CONTENTS

NOTES ON CONTRIBUTORS

1. Robin Means is a Research Fellow at the School for Advanced Urban Studies, University of Bristol.

2. Lyn Harrison is a Research Associate at the School for Advanced Urban Studies, University of Bristol.

3. Debbie Clarke is a freelance management and training consultant and a Visiting Lecturer at the School for Advanced Urban Studies, University of Bristol.

4. Kevin Doogan is a Research Associate at the School for Advanced Urban Studies, University of Bristol.

5. Derek Close is a freelance training consultant and regional training consultant to the South West alcohol education programme.

6. Barbara Howe is a Research Fellow at the Drugs Addiction Unit, School of Education, University of Durham.

ACKNOWLEDGEMENTS

We would like to acknowledge our indebtedness to all the people who kindly completed the questionnaires for our evaluation of the 'Drinking Choices' courses in the South West.

Mark Cox here at the School has provided us with advice on how to handle the data and carried out the various tasks associated with this: we are most grateful to him for his assistance.

We would like to thank Julie Platt and Pam Aldren in the School's Publications Department who have provided their usual invaluable help in the production of this paper.

Our research is funded by the Health Education Council but the views in this paper are entirely those of the authors.

Robin Means
Lyn Harrison

INTRODUCTION

Between 1965 and 1980 total world production of alcohol rose by almost 50%, two thirds of it being produced in Europe and North America. Between 1962 and 1982, Britain has seen a 24% rise in wine drinking, a 95% rise in spirit drinking and a 22% rise in beer drinking.[1] The most common reason given for this increase being that the real price of most alcoholic drinks in Britain has fallen at a time when the real personal disposable income per head has risen.[2]

The consequences of these trends for a variety of health and social problems has recently been illustrated by reports from the Royal College of Psychiatrists[3] and the Royal College of General Practitioners.[4] Both reports agree that the vast majority of these problems are not generated by a small minority of very excessive drinkers who are open to the label of being an 'alcoholic'. As explained in the report of the Royal College of Psychiatrists:

> The more an individual habitually drinks, the greater the likelihood of developing cirrhosis, of being involved in accidents, of losing his job, of becoming physically dependent on alcohol and so on. But a substantial proportion of the ill effects are generated by quite moderate drinkers. A young man may drown swimming in the sea, or crash his car, simply because he has unwisely drunk four pints of beer for lunch, and a middle-aged woman may suffer burns when she falls deeply asleep after three whiskies and neglects her lighted cigarette. The chances of their doing so are small in comparison with those who drink two or three times as much. But because relatively moderate drinkers are so much more numerous than those who drink a bottle of gin or ten pints of beer a day, between them they still account for a high proportion of the ill effects.[5]

Various prevention strategies are available to government to reduce the indices of alcohol related harm. These include fiscal measures, restrictions on alcohol advertising and public education campaigns. There is also the option of training the professionals since "as awareness of the importance of alcohol problems increases each professional group should be expected to give prominence to alcohol problems in its own curricula in both undergraduate and post-qualifying courses".[6]

One of the organisations responsible for public and professional education about alcohol has been the Health Education Council (HEC). The HEC was a quango that was 100% financed by the Department of Health and Social Security. On 1 April, 1987, it was reconstituted into the Health Education Authority which will be an integral part of the National Health Service and directly accountable to the Secretary of State for Social Services. Since March 1984, the HEC has been funding what is known as the South West alcohol education programme. The editors of this publication are members of the evaluation team who are studying the impact of this programme.

The central thrust of the South West programme is primary prevention and a central activity has been professional training. The intention is that these professionals will continue the work of primary prevention in the South West long after the formal life of the programme. One task for the evaluation team has, therefore, been to assess the extent to which this programme has fostered the introduction of alcohol education and associated measures where none existed before, and above all changes in the amount or style of education.

The main mechanism for assessing this will be four locality studies that reflect something of the diversity of the region. The four localities chosen were:

1.   a market town together with a nearby tourist/fishing village;

2.   a market town which was the administrative centre for its county;

3.   a group of isolated villages;

4.   a large inter war council housing estate in a large urban connurbation.

Between 30 and 55 meetings were held with statutory and voluntary sector professionals in each of these areas. Each respondent was asked about their level of involvement in alcohol education and how this related to organisational role, professional training and perceived local drinking patterns and problems.[7]

These four studies provided a detailed account of alcohol education structures at the initial stages of the programme. It will, therefore, be possible to return to these areas at a later date to assess what impact the programme has had upon activity at the local level through interviewing the same respondents. Have most respondents been aware of or influenced by the programme? Have they taken part in any alcohol education initiatives? etc.

One mechanism by which a growing number of professionals will be drawn into alcohol education in the South West is through the professional training strategy of the programme. This publication evolved out of the collective efforts by both researchers and trainers associated with the South West programme to respond to some of the difficulties that have been encountered by this strategy. Our hope is that the various chapters and contributors will enable the reader to think through the needs of their own organisation for training in alcohol education.

References

1.   **Smith, R.** (1987) The national politics of alcohol education, School for Advanced Urban Studies, University of Bristol, Working Paper No 66.

2.   **Kendall, R.** (1979) 'Alcoholism: a medical or a political problem?', British Medical Journal, Vol 1, No 6160, pp 369-370.

3.   **Royal College of Psychiatrists** (1986) Alcohol - our favourite drug, Tavistock: London.

4.   **Royal College of General Practitioners** (1986) Alcohol - a balanced view, The College.

5.   **Royal College of Psychiatrist** (op cit), p 110.

6.   **Ibid,** p 31.

7.   **Means, R., Harrison, L., Hoyes, L., and Smith, R.** (1986) Educating about alcohol: professional perspectives and practice in South West England, School for Advanced Urban Studies, University of Bristol, Occasional Paper No 25.

1

THE DEVELOPMENT OF A TRAINING STRATEGY FOR ALCOHOL EDUCATION IN SOUTH WEST ENGLAND

Lyn Harrison and Robin Means

Introduction

The purpose of this chapter is to describe the development of a training strategy for alcohol educators by the South West alcohol education programme. Following chapters will not only further explore the 'success' or 'failure' of that strategy from a research perspective, but also illustrate how such strategies can be amended through the developmental learning of trainers, whether operating at a national or local level.

This chapter begins by providing a brief outline of the South West alcohol education programme. This is followed by a consideration of the influence of the previous North East or Tyne Tees alcohol education campaign, particularly with regard to professional training. The third section describes the training plan laid down for such professionals in the Action Plan of the South West alcohol education programme, and then discusses why this was beset with certain implementation problems from the outset. The final section outlines the rest of the contributions to this publication.

The South West alcohol education programme

The South West alcohol education programme is primarily funded by the Health Education Council (HEC). The programme came into existence in April 1984 and was initially expected to run for three years until March 1987. A two year extension to the programme until March 1989 was granted in September 1986.

For the purposes of this programme, the HEC saw the South Western Regional Health Authority area as the most appropriate operational definition of the region. It was also decided to include Bath District Health Authority, much of which is within Avon, and the West Dorset Health Authority area, which in terms of television coverage is part of the South West. Thus the region as defined by this educational programme covers the five counties of Cornwall, Devon, Somerset, Avon and Gloucestershire, plus a part of Wiltshire and a part of Dorset. In other words, a very large area indeed, and a very complex one in terms of administrative boundaries. For example, there are 13 District Health Authorities and seven different Councils on Alcoholism.

A Regional Co-ordinator was appointed in April 1984 and was based at the Avon Council on Alcoholism in Bristol. A Deputy Co-ordinator was appointed in September 1984 and was based at the Devon Council on Alcoholism in Exeter. The initially chosen research team decided not to proceed with the opportunity to evaluate the South West programme and a new team was not established until November 1984. The new team was based at the School for Advanced Urban Studies, University of Bristol and included the two editors of this publication.

The first two years of the South West alcohol education programme have proved to be difficult for a number of complex reasons. The Co-ordinator and Deputy Co-ordinator were trying to develop a regional programme over a very large geographical area and with limited financial resources. Support was potentially available from a variety of sources, namely the HEC in London, the research team, their immediate employers (two different Councils on Alcoholism), a Regional Advisory Committee of over 30 members and a Planning and Monitoring Group of seven members. There was uncertainty about the respective roles of these various groups. Impossible demands were placed on the programme staff. The Co-ordinator resigned in April 1985 and the Deputy Co-ordinator in September 1985.

There was wide agreement that the original arrangements were unsatisfactory. The Planning and Monitoring Group agreed to take on a clearer and stronger management role and the HEC agreed to increase its staffing support in London for all its alcohol and drug education activities. It was decided to develop the South West programme mainly at District Health Authority (DHA) level through the appointment of a rolling programme of local co-ordinators. These posts have usually been 50% funded by the HEC. At the time of writing, eight are in post; six of them are based in the Health Education Units of DHAs and two are based in local Councils on Alcoholism. A new Regional Co-ordinator was appointed in June 1986 and the postholder is located in the Regional Health Authority.

Prior to their resignations, the Co-ordinators had produced an Action Plan and Information Pack in Spring 1985 that became the basis for a whole series of local briefing conferences on the South West alcohol education programme. In the Action Plan, the overall approach to the programme was seen as having four key points. First, the progamme would be about promoting health, and sensible drinking was seen as potentially one aspect of a healthy life style, although so was the option to be a non-drinker. Second, the programme was not going to use a medical or disease model of alcoholism[1] but rather sought to encourage informed debate about the part alcohol plays in the lives of individuals and aimed to help people to understand what sensible drinking meant to them through an awareness of influences at the individual, social and cultural levels. Third, the Action Plan stressed that the emphasis of the programme was on primary prevention and thus relevant to the whole population. And finally, the programme would seek to promote action and change at all levels so that it was targeted at "policy makers and planners, at managers, at trainers and educators, as well as the individual person".[2] These themes were reflected in the chosen title for the programme, Understanding Alcohol.

The Action Plan explained that it was difficult to be precise about target groups because this was going to be an active developmental programme. However, it was suggested that the initial target group might be health promoters since "one clear priority has emerged" and that was "the need for a major and intensive programme of education for the workers in field level organisations who are in direct contact with the public".[3] It was also suggested that two other groups should be prioritised, namely young people and people at their place of work. This training programme for professionals was to be based on the Drinking Choices Manual[4] which was developed by Ina Simnett, Linda Wright and Martin Evans for the Health Education Council and the Teachers' Advisory Council on Alcohol and Drug Education (TACADE). This training manual had evolved from the previous Tyne Tees alcohol education campaign.

The Tyne Tees alcohol education campaign and the Drinking Choices Manual

The previous Tyne Tees education campaign was also funded by the HEC. A pilot campaign was launched in the North East of England in 1974 with the following objectives:

1. To increase public and professional awareness of alcohol and its problems.
2. To establish the feasibility of health education about alcohol and its problems.[5]

This pilot campaign was media based and mainly concerned with getting problem drinkers to come forward for treatment. One of the main problems identified with this campaign "was the lack of back-up facilities to counsel and support those who came forward with a drink problem or to seek help for a relative or friend who had a drink problem".[6]

Funding for a second phase was not found until 1977/78 and this also had a strong media element, although this time geared towards primary prevention and encouraging sensible drinking. More specifically the campaign in the period 1981-84 focused around the 'Why spoil a good thing' television advertisements by David Bellamy. These activities were evaluated by a research team from the Centre for Mass Communications Research, University of Leicester. The effects of the David Bellamy advertisements were quite encouraging in terms of conveying specific information on the target audience but the research team warned that "any campaign which affected the general public but failed to mobilise professionals who, on their own admission, knew little about the subject, would be doomed to achieve very limited 'effectiveness'".[7]

However, the campaign after 1977, also, had strong non media components, partly because of what had been learnt from phase one which sparked off a demand for counselling that could not be met. A community education programme was to be carried out by alcohol educators and sustained by the local Health Education Units as part of their health education activities. Health education officers were to be trained "in effective ways of supporting the campaigns"[8] and this would include gaining the skills to train a wide range of professional groups in alcohol education.

However, the problem which emerged from this programme of action was that the regional co-ordinating group, responsible for organising the training seminars for professionals, found that the responsibility for running alcohol education activities was not taken up by others but remained with this group. The group therefore in 1979 asked a team of three health education officers (HEOs) to produce a module which could be used to train multi-disciplinary groups as alcohol educators through one week courses. The training manual was devised and informally evaluated and then re-written and printed to be used in a regional training programme by 1981. This regional initiative to train alcohol educators was evaluated by a research worker, Donna Brandes, on behalf of the HEC. Unfortunately, the resultant report is only available as an unpublished PhD, entitled <u>An illuminative evaluation of an alcohol education project.</u>[9]

The evaluation carried out by Brandes was to assess both the impact of the <u>Drinking Choices Manual</u> and its method of dissemination within the North East. The manual and the model of dissemination had been devised so that the knowledge and skills of a small number of experts could be acquired by a wide range of individuals drawn from a variety of backgrounds.

10 specific aims are listed in the manual which states that on completion of the course, students will:

1. Hold the attitude that education can be an effective means of prevention.

2. Have confidence in their ability as alcohol educators.

3. Take action by educating their clients about alcohol.

4. Be able to use and apply their previous experience, training and knowledge to alcohol education.

5. Be able to see the needs of the whole person in relation to their life situation and identify the way alcohol fits into this picture.

6. Be able to apply educational strategies to alcohol problems at primary, secondary and tertiary levels of prevention.

7. Have knowledge about the development of an individual's drinking behaviour and how it is influenced by social, legal, cultural, economic, psychological and genetic factors.

8. Have knowledge of the influence on drinking patterns in our society of cultural, economic, fiscal, legal and educational factors.

9. Have knowledge about the biochemical and pharmacological properties of alcohol and its part in the host-agent-environment system.

10.   Be aware of, and understand, current theories
       about alcohol use and abuse.[10]

Some other important characteristics of the manual are that
course members are expected to explore their own attitudes and
experiences before engaging with other people on alcohol issues;
the manual is to be used with multi-disciplinary groups so as to
encourage common understanding.   The educational approach on
which the manual is based is a participatory learning method. One
significant outcome of this style of learning is that all course
members and their views are equally respected; the course is not
about expert leaders teaching the correct view on alcohol and
drinking.

The manual offers an extremely detailed training plan.   Each
activity has a title, a number, a stated objective and a time
allowance together with an indication of organisation, method and
content.   The suggested main activities for each day are listed in
Table 1.   The bulk of these activities are addressed in a
participative manner.   For example, there is a 30 minute exercise
called 'Why do people drink?'[11] on day two. Three objectives are
listed for this activity:

(a)   to understand that there are a wide range of
       reasons why people drink;

(b)   to understand that the personal rewards from
       drinking are similar to other activities (eg sport);

(c)   to identify basic human needs that can be met by
       either drinking or sport.

Under 'organisation, method and content', this activity is further
broken down into the following five components:

(a)   Working in groups of three or four, ask students to
       list the rewards, or 'pay-offs' that people gain
       from (a) sport (b) drinking.

(b)   Trainer builds up two lists of rewards on
       OHP/flipchart from the small groups'
       contributions.

Table 1: Main activities in the teaching plan of the Drinking Choices Manual

Day One

(a) Introduction
(b) Alcohol: what do you know?
(c) Review and update
(d) Blood alcohol exercise
(e) Why educate about alcohol?
(f) Small group project
(g) Self-assessment exercise
(h) Homework

Day Two

(a) Warm-up exercise
(b) Key facts
(c) Why do people drink?
(d) Social norms and attitudes related to drinking
(e) Drinking values continuum exercise
(f) Milling with labels
(g) A terminology of drinkers
(h) Aims of alcohol education
(i) Small group project
(j) Introduction to research project on agencies
(k) Homework

Day Three

(a) Warm-up exercise
(b) Drinking careers
(c) Road map exercise
(d) Social norms and attitudes (continued)
(e) The Karpman Triangle
(f) Active listening
(g) Film: 15 today
(h) Small group project
(i) Homework

Day Four

(a) Warm-up exercise
(b) Feedback from homework
(c) Alcohol and the law
(d) Use of visual aids
(e) Assessing written material
(f) Review of resources for alcohol education
(g) Small group project
(h) Report on defining the problem
(i) Homework

Day Five

(a) Warm-up exercise
(b) Research findings re drinking careers
(c) Reports of research projects on agencies
(d) The Tyne Tees alcohol campaign
(e) Small group project
(f) Self-assessment exercise
(g) Personal contracts

11

(c)   As a full group, discuss similarities and differences between the two lists.

(d)   Ask group to identify the basic human needs that are being met by sport and drinking.

(e)   Point out to the group that if they or others want to change either their drinking patterns or their involvement in sport, then it is important to find alternative ways for getting what they need. Ask them briefly for possible alternatives.

Besides the detailed teaching plan, the manual also contains separate sections of students' material and of trainers' material that will be used during the various activities.

The knowledge and skills acquired by the course participants as a result of this very intensive input were seen as appropriate for anyone acting as an alcohol educator, whether with clients, family or colleagues and also could enable particular professionals to provide an educational component in the treatment of problem drinkers. The method by which these skills and knowledge were to be disseminated within the North East was also clearly identified within the Drinking Choices Manual:

> We envisage a domino effect in the spread of learning and skills from the writers of the manual, to the health education officers, from them to the alcohol educators, and from the educators to their own clients.[12]

In more specific terms for the North East this process was seen as a pyramid of learning by the research evaluator as can be seen from Table 2.

It can be seen from this table that the dissemination process started with courses being run for HEOs so that they could train other trainers. Thus the people involved in Level I and Level II of the pyramid were explicitly involved in training in their professional roles. These professionals would then continue the dissemination process into their own organisations by running courses for their colleagues and clients. It was the individuals trained at Level III who then would become the major interface with the general public. It appears then from this model that the manual is a tool which can be used to produce trainers, counsellors and educators in the context of alcohol and drinking.

12

Table 2: Pyramid 1: dissemination plans for DCM

LEVEL 1
Sept 81-Feb 82
(Seven districts represented)

Alcohol Project is initiated by Regional Sub-Committee for alcohol campaign

Initial training course for health education officers Northumberland, Durham, Newcastle, Cleveland, North and South Tyneside, Sunderland, Gateshead

LEVEL II
Series A: Jun 82-Jun 83
Series B: Dec 82-Dec 82

HEOs train other trainers
Professional colleagues: nurses, tutors, other HEOs, workers in the health service, etc

LEVEL III

Trainers use the module with professional colleagues and clients. Courses are organised for social workers, probation officers, educators, nurses, youth and community workers

LEVEL IV

Trainers use the module with members of the general public. Courses will be offered and advertised throughout the North East to members of the public, schools, adult education, clinics, hospitals, etc as well as information contact of professionals with members of the general public

(Source: **Brandes, D. V.** (1985), <u>An illuminative evaluation of an alcohol education project</u>, PhD thesis, University of Durham, p 13.)

In practice then how did this model of dissemination work? The data collected and analysed by Brandes indicated that in general the actual manual was well received by the majority of course members. It was felt to be very adaptable and for many professionals rapidly became "part of their repertoire of responses to the need for health education".[13] One of the most successful outcomes related to the manual was the establishment of inter-disciplinary links which went as far as the formation of community alcohol teams in some health districts.[14] The manual was seen as an effective means of training a large number of people to become alcohol educators. However, Brandes did uncover major problems with the 'cascade' model of implementation.

The 'cascade' model did seem to work at the upper end of the pyramid. This applied in particular to the skills acquired by HEOs in participatory methods of teaching. However, even they had to be given extra support from a training 'expert' before they felt able to run their own full Drinking Choices Manual (DCM) courses. Given this, it was perhaps not surprising that the pyramid only operated as far as Level II and no complete DCM courses were run at Level III. The failure at this stage was in part due to professionals attending courses for their own personal development, their course organisers having failed to make it clear that there was an expectation they should become trainers. However, in many cases it was the blocks professionals experienced within their own organisations that prevented them running training courses for other professionals.

Although Level III was omitted some professionals did pass on directly their knowledge and skills to their clients, representing Level IV of the pyramid model. Interestingly the people impacted at Level IV tended to represent very particular groups of people identified either because of specific drink problems or other social problems. Professionals working with these groups would, in general, be using one to one counselling skills. The main exception to this emphasis on problem individuals or families was the work carried out with students and pupils where a wider educational approach was more likely to be used. Again it would appear that 'the cascade' of skills and knowledge only permeated part of the anticipated network. Members of the public were reached only insomuch as they were 'a captive audience' available to specific professional workers.

This tension in the focus of the manual is reflected in the evaluator's report when she states that the DCM "is at best an effective educational programme and can be used as such in providing services for prevention and treatment of alcohol problems".[15] She supports this statement with a quotation from Grant and Ritson:

> The current state of treatment research suggests that heavy demands in the immediate future are likely to be placed on education. The task is to raise the overall level of understanding about alcohol and its effects, to enhance recognition of harmful drinking both in the mind of the sufferers and those whom they encounter and to reduce the stigma and misunderstanding which surround our knowledge of alcoholism.[16]

This does seem to leave a strong emphasis on the role of the DCM in helping professionals in their work with problem drinkers and their families and friends. Would this become an issue when DCM was applied to the South West programme with its very clear and unambiguous focus on primary prevention?

The training strategy of the South West alcohol education programme

As already indicated the HEC programme in South West England is entitled Understanding Alcohol and is essentially concerned with primary prevention. A training programme for potential health promoters was seen by the Action Plan as essential to the eventual success of the overall endeavour.

The Action Plan explained that this programme would be based on the Drinking Choices Manual and that courses would be run targeted at what were called 'key tutors'. Key tutors were defined as being either professional or voluntary workers with existing training responsibilities in the area of alcohol or health education. Again a pyramid model of dissemination was envisaged:

South West Alcohol Programme Co-ordinator

⌐Key tutors⌐

⌐Alcohol educators⌐

⌐Clients Clients Clients Clients Clients Clients⌐ [17]

15

The Regional Co-ordinator and Deputy Co-ordinator intended to run such 'Drinking Choices' courses throughout the region. This would produce a network of key tutors in the South West who would in turn run courses for alcohol educators. These alcohol educators, through their work with a wide range of client groups, would have an impact on the general public. Such courses were seen by the Action Plan as offering "a coherent model which can be used to integrate prevention and treatment and which provides impetus for primary and secondary prevention".[18] The key tutors in the South West had an equivalent role to the HEOs at Level I in the pyramid of dissemination in the North East. The key tutors were to be "in a position and have the time and be free to run 'Drinking Choices' courses". In addition, they were already to possess skills as trainers and "be interested in the broad field of education for life/life and social skills education/personal and social education/health promotion".[19] The key tutors should also be interested in developing a role in the South West programme and in working on an inter-disciplinary basis. While one group of potential key tutors was health education officers, another 20 professional groups were also identified as being capable of fulfilling this role.

While a network of key tutors was envisaged extending throughout the region it was hoped that this would be based on a local team within each health district. These teams would continue to be supported after the training course through follow up events and other links organised by the programme's co-ordinators.

The rationale behind this training programme clearly reflected the original 'cascade' model from the North East. The Regional Co-ordinator for the South West programme having been involved in the development of the Drinking Choices Manual was a key link between the two programmes. Unfortunately, the chosen strategy possessed many of the same tensions. The programme was directed towards primary prevention and so could potentially engage with anyone, whatever her or his drinking pattern, and the key tutors were to support this philosophy and be interested in the wider aspect of health and social education. However, the Drinking Choices Manual can be used to develop trainers, alcohol educators and counsellors. The programme needed trainers with a commitment to primary prevention to support its philosophy but used a training manual which was valuable for professionals operating across the spectrum in relation to alcohol issues and which acknowledged the importance of everyone's perspective. Thus the recruitment to the courses became critical in determining in what roles individuals used the skills and knowledge they acquired through the training programme in the South West. In other words, a careful targeting of these courses towards trainers and those with strong primary prevention interests would be crucial as would the capacity to attract professionals who related to the programme priority groups of young people and the workplace.

At the time of writing (November 1986), six such courses have been run for 90 participants and a further two are planned. The first course was held in Falmouth in October 1984 for 18 participants and this was followed by courses in Taunton in January 1985 for 18 people and in May 1985 for 13 people. The fourth course for 13 participants took place in Exeter in October 1985 and a fifth for 15 was held in Bristol in February 1986. In addition, 13 people attended a shorter three day course for North Devon professionals in late 1985.

Table 3 indicates that these courses have not been very successful at achieving an even distribution of key tutors throughout the region.

Table 3:   The geographical spread of key tutors

Number of key tutors

Devon	34 (13 of these on separate North Devon three day course)
Avon	17
Somerset	12
Cornwall	11
Dorset	10
Gloucestershire	3
Wiltshire	3

This seems at odds with the emphasis of the Action Plan upon the importance of local networks of alcohol educators built around key tutors.

Table 4 gives a breakdown of all those that attended the first six courses based on the postal questionnaires described later in this chapter. It can be seen from the outset that these early courses were composed of a wide range of professional groups and the balance of these groups varied considerably from course to course. Why did this happen and does it imply a lack of any kind of targeting strategy from programme staff?

17

Table 4: Key tutors by professional group

CATEGORY	Falmouth course Oct 84	Taunton course one Jan 85	Taunton course two May 85	Exeter Oct 85	Bristol Feb 86	North Devon (3 days)	TOTALS
(i) Community worker, youth worker	-	2	-	3	-	2	7
(ii) General practitioner	-	1	1	-	-	-	2
(iii) Health education officer	2	4	1	-	3	1	11
(iv) Health visitor	-	-	-	-	1	-	1
(v) Hospital doctor and para medics	2	-	-	-	1	1	4
(vi) Nurse/nurse tutor	1	4	2	1	-	1	9
(vii) Personnel/welfare officer	1	-	1	1	-	-	3
(viii) Police officer/prison officer	2	-	1	-	-	1	4
(ix) Probation	2	-	3	1	2	2	10
(x) School teacher/head teacher	2	-	2	5	2	1	12
(xi) Social worker/manager/trainer	-	3	1	-	-	1	5
(xii) Voluntary counsellor	2	2	-	-	-	-	4
(xiii) Self employed	-	-	-	2	1	-	3
(xiv) Voluntary sector manager	4	2	1	-	3	1	11
(xv) Other	-	-	-	-	2	2	4
TOTALS	18	18	13	13	15	13	90

The first point to make is that both the Regional Co-ordinator and Deputy Co-ordinator found themselves under enormous work pressure almost from the start. For example, the Regional Co-ordinator was not only trying to co-ordinate the programme but was also expected to run these residential events each of which was split into two separate three day sessions. She did not feel able to delay their running until later in the programme because then she risked the allegation that she had not trained educators who could respond to the programme when it was more formally launched in the region in mid-1985. As a result, she decided to run the first three events (Falmouth and the two Taunton courses) in late 1984 and early 1985, which was before a decision was made to accept young people and the workplace as priority areas for the programme. One response of the Regional and Deputy Co-ordinators to these pressures was to place a heavy reliance upon both Health Education Units and Councils on Alcoholism to 'spread the word' about the existence of the first three courses.

However, the nature of both these organisations differed in the South West compared to the North East, and in both cases this was probably to the disadvantage of the South West alcohol education programme. Brandes states in her evaluation that HEOs in the North East "have a long history of working well together, for at least a decade".[20] When the South West alcohol education programme arrived in the region there were very few DHEOs in post. In any case the geographical spread of the region is notorious for hindering professional groups within the South Western Regional Health Authority (SWRHA) developing a strong collective identity. The SWRHA itself has tended, perhaps also reflecting the geography of the region, to have a less intimate and directive relationship with its districts than other Regional Health Authorities.

In addition during the early stages of the programme many HEOs were coming into post and were pre-occupied with the immediate task of establishing their units.[21] This meant that unlike the HEOs in the North East the Co-ordinator in the South West could not expect the HEOs to be able to respond to another external demand and provide an established network of inter organisational links for disseminating and supporting the programme.

Within the South West region there were already seven established Councils on Alcoholism. These had very different histories, structures and styles of operating and, like many voluntary organisations, while dependent on other agencies to maintain their funding, were fiercely protective of their independence.[22] In the North East there was only a single Council on Alcoholism and this was established alongside the HEC programme, and indeed initially part funded by the HEC.

Many of the Councils in the South West had for a long period of time been the only agency providing an alcohol advisory service. This meant that Councils were involved in a mixture of activities, including counselling problem drinkers, educational sessions in a variety of settings and providing a resource and information service. Many Councils if supported by extra resources were eager to extend their educational and training activities and felt they were the key agency with the experience to develop this work in the alcohol field.

The close link between the HEC programme and the Council on Alcoholism in the North East was initiated through the pilot programme which was ambivalent about its central focus being on primary or secondary prevention. The evaluation by the Centre for Mass Communication Research also points to the uncertainty about the extent to which the initial phase of the campaign was based on the disease model of alcoholism. However, the later stages of the North East campaign and the South West programme were unambiguously focused on primary prevention and supporting sensible drinking, not necessarily abstinence.

The relationship of some Councils on Alcoholism in the South West to an educational programme based on this philosophy was difficult. Some Councils felt that alcohol education could only start from the recognition of the damage caused by alcohol in certain people's lives. Alcohol education was about recognising problems and preventing people becoming damaged. This is very different from approaching alcohol education as part of a social education programme designed to enhance self respect and the ability to carry out informed decision making.

However, despite the different ways in which some Health Education Units (HEUs) and some Councils on Alcoholism had problems in supporting the South West programme, the Regional Co-ordinator was initially dependent on these points of contact, reflecting as they did both the potential and actual pools of commitment and expertise in respect of alcohol education. Thus the membership of the first three 'Drinking Choices' courses, one in Falmouth and two in Taunton, reflects the process of recruitment which took place through the contacts of the Councils on

20

Alcoholism and the existing HEUs. Seven of the total 11 HEOs trained and 11 of the 15 voluntary sector counsellors or managers attended these courses.

By the time the fourth training course was run at Exeter the programme was being organised by its Planning and Monitoring Group. It was fortunate then that one of this group attended the Exeter course and because of his expertise in the area of young people and education enabled the course to target teaching professionals more directly. This made the selection of key tutors more effectively directed to one of the two priority groups identified in the Action Plan, namely young people. As already indicated, this period also saw a restructuring of the programme towards a more decentralised approach based on local co-ordinators working from District Health Authorities. The final two courses reflected this focus. A three day event was organised for North Devon professionals in which the district health education officer brought together a group of local professionals who wanted to tackle alcohol education issues. Finally, the first two local co-ordinators to come into post were based in different parts of Avon and they recruited two small groups of interested local professionals for the Bristol course. These could then form the basis of a local network of key tutors.

Targeting these courses effectively to achieve the training strategy laid down in the Action Plan has proved difficult. The first problem was over-stretched programme staff. The second difficulty was staff resignations. Later courses have improved on targeting but there remained a tension between targeting towards the priority groups (the Exeter course) and targeting to achieve active local networks (the Bristol course).

The other contributions

Chapter 1 has looked at the development of a training strategy for alcohol educators in South West England and some of the factors that influenced the nature of recruitment. Considerable tensions were seen to exist between the strategy and some of those attracted to the early DCM courses. The Planning and Monitoring Group of the South West alcohol education programme was also aware of many of these problems and this group was particularly concerned that many key tutors might not be going on to become active alcohol educators through the running of events and the establishment of local networks of key tutors. This group was, therefore, keen for some detailed research to be carried out by the

SAUS evaluation team on course participants. The evaluation team had originally intended to focus down on key tutors only insofar as they were based within one of four detailed locality case studies.[23] However, in autumn 1985, it was agreed to respond to the Planning and Monitoring Group, by developing a series of postal questionnaires for each course participant (see Appendix). These would be administered just before (Questionnaire I) and just after (Questionnaire II) course attendance to test the immediate impact of being on a 'Drinking Choices' course. A third questionnaire (Questionnaire III) would be administered after six months and at regular intervals thereafter in order to trace the subsequent alcohol education careers of participants, with a particular focus on whether they have gone on to run their own full courses. Since these questionnaires were not available until early 1987, a considerable amount of data from the early course participants had to be collected retrospectively with all the obvious limitations this creates in terms of reliability of response. A shortened questionnaire that combined some elements of Questionnaires I and II was used for this purpose.

Research on key tutors in the South West is continuing so that this publication represents some preliminary and tentative findings. These findings are outlined in Chapter 3 by Kevin Doogan who analyses the early data that has been received back from the questionnaires. The central focus of this chapter is whether the pyramid identified in the Action Plan was being developed by key tutors after leaving their courses but it also reflects upon other aspects of being an active key tutor. Kevin Doogan was asked by the editors to produce a chapter based only on data within the questionnaire and not influenced by the kind of contextual information on recruitment provided in the previous section of this chapter. Chapter 2 is by Debbie Clarke who was commissioned by the research team to attend one of these courses as a participant observer. Her contribution reflects on the strengths and weaknesses of the six day residential course as a base for future activity as an alcohol trainer or educator.

The next two chapters switch the focus from a research perspective to a training perspective and both illustrate the capacity of skilled trainers to adapt packages such as the Drinking Choices Manual to meet their needs and those of course members. In Chapter 4, Derek Close, who has been the training consultant to the programme since the resignation of the Regional Co-ordinator, reflects on his own flexible use of DCM. He explains how he has tried to meet the needs of local co-ordinators, why he decided to run shorter three day events and why there is a need to sometimes amend the use of the manual to reflect the needs of particular professional groups. In Chapter 5, Barbara Howe offers her perspective as the HEC funded national disseminator for 'Drinking Choices' courses and she explains how her learning from this has been incorporated into a new drugs training manual.

In the final chapter, the editors reflect on these various contributions and try to draw out the most important themes and issues that need to be borne in mind by those who in the future will try to promote this kind of approach to professional education in alcohol and drugs.

References

1. For a detailed discussion of the limitations of the disease model of alcoholism see **Heather, N. and Robertson, I.** (1985), Problem drinking: the new approach, Harmondsworth: Penguin, especially Chapter 4.

2. **South West alcohol education programme** (1985) Action Plan: understanding alcohol, Health Education Council, para 2.1.2.

3. **Ibid.**

4. **Simnett, I., Wright, L. and Evans, M.** (1982) Drinking Choices: a training manual for alcohol educators, TACADE/HEC.

5. Quoted in **Budd, J., Gray, P., and McCron, R.** (1982) The Tyne Tees alcohol education campaign: an evaluation, Health Education Council, London, p 26.

6. **Simnett, et al,** op cit, p 117.

7. **Budd, et al,** op cit, p 96.

8. **Brandes, D.** (1985) An illuminative evaluation of an alcohol education project, PhD Thesis, University of Durham, p 10.

9. **Brandes,** op cit.

10. **Simnett, et al,** op cit, p 6.

11. **Ibid,** p 23.

12. **Ibid,** p 6.

13. **Brandes,** op cit, p 246.

14. **Ibid,** p 360.

15. **Ibid,** p 183.

16. **Grant, M.** and **Ritson, B.** (1983) <u>Alcohol: the prevention debate</u>, London: Croom Helm, quoted in **Brandes,** op cit.

17. **South West alcohol education programme,** op cit, para 4.2.3.

18. **Ibid.**

19. **Ibid.**

20. **Brandes,** op cit, p 178.

21. This issue is developed further in **Harrison, L.** and **Means, R.** (1986) 'Implementing an holistic approach to alcohol education', <u>Health Education Journal</u>, Vol 45, No 3, pp 132-136.

22. See, also **Means, R., Harrison, L., Hoyes, L.** and **Smith, R.** (1985) <u>Educating about alcohol: professional perspectives and practice in South West England</u>, School for Advanced Urban Studies, University of Bristol, Occasional Paper No 25, especially Chapter 6.

23. The first phase of the locality case study research is written up in **Means, et al,** op cit.

2

BECOMING AN ALCOHOL EDUCATOR: A PARTICIPANT OBSERVER PERSPECTIVE

Debbie Clarke

Introduction

This chapter documents my experience, as a participant, on the 'Drinking Choices' course, run on 5-7 February and 25-26 February 1986 in Bristol. It outlines my views as to the particular strengths and weaknesses of this course and makes recommendations as to the ways in which the course could be improved. The course was organised as part of the HEC's alcohol education programme in the South West of England. The course tutors were Derek Close, the training consultant for the programme and Barbara Howe, Research Fellow for the HEC Addictions Project based at the School of Education, University of Durham.

I am a freelance management and training consultant, and a Visiting Lecturer at University of Bristol, with experience in working in the alcohol field. I have been involved in training work since 1978, and have qualifications in Counselling, Social Work and Consultancy. I worked at an alcohol treatment unit, 1980-1981 in Bristol, and trained the volunteer counsellors at the Avon Council on Alcoholism for four years. I was a founder member of DAWN (Bristol) which is Drug, Alcohol, Women Nationally, a campaigning organisation looking at women and dependency. I am at present involved on a research project funded by the MSC to look at participative learning in YTS. I also run courses in participative learning for professionals.

There were 15 participants on the 'Drinking Choices' course. Two were local co-ordinators for the South West alcohol education programme and both were based in Health Education Units. There was a health visitor, a psychologist, and a volunteer organiser for a NHS hospital. One participant worked at a drugs advisory service and another for a private drug treatment clinic. There were two probation officers, three lecturers from technical colleges or colleges of higher education, a youth worker, a road safety officer and a therapist. These course members were unaware of my research task although they were subsequently informed by letter. At the time, they perceived me as just another course member although both course tutors were aware of the real situation.

My individual experience of the course

1. Pre-course information

It is difficult for me to assess the extent to which the participants had a clear idea about the nature of the course prior to the event. For myself, however, the first written communication I received was a letter from the tutors outlining the course and giving me details regarding the location. There was little information regarding the aims and objectives for the course, or the role I might be required to play during or after the event. What was said was:

> The course will be of a participative nature with a minimum of inputs from tutors. Much of the work will be carried out in groups using materials from the Drinking Choices Manual and you will be asked to present material and exercises from the manual during the course. The tutors' role will be one of supporter, facilitator and resourcer and provider of frameworks.

Unless I had been well briefed, prior to this letter, I would not have had an understanding of the concept of key tutor,[1] and the extent to which I might be expected to develop a training role, upon completion of the course. The only mention made in the letter was as follows:

> There is an expectation that you will be able to devote some of your time to alcohol education during the next two years.

2. Arrival, registration, introductions

The registration was handled well, and the location staff were welcoming and efficient.

3. Course introductions

The introduction to the course went well. The tutors set the scene and style of the course. They managed to put the participants at ease, by engaging in a number of introductory exercises, which were informative without being threatening. They worked well together, presenting a good balance of experience, knowledge, and training style. Their approach contradicted some stereotypes, in that the male tutor had a tendency to be involved with 'process', and the female tutor identified as having greater 'product' knowledge.

4.   Clarifying objectives, and the style of the course

Participants were given an opportunity to share with each other, and the tutors, their expectations or 'wants' from the course. The tutors commented upon these, and stated the extent to which these expectations were realistic, given the overall objectives for the course. It was at this point that I felt insufficent time was given to putting the course into context, particularly with respect to the Understanding Alcohol programme, and the role of key tutor. Valuable time could have been spent here, I feel, in allowing participants to make any necessary links, and in clarifying their position with relation to their willingness to run future events.

5.   Introduction to the Drinking Choices Manual

The DCM was introduced after lunch on the first day, in a low key, non-threatening way.   At first sight, however, it is a rather impressive looking document, and I along with a number of other participants was quite intimidated by the idea that we would be expected to become familiar and feel confident with such a large amount of information.   My anxieties were not alleviated when I was asked to read the aims for the course, which are reproduced below.

On completion of the course students will:

(a)   Hold the attitude that education can be an effective means of prevention.

(b)   Have confidence in their ability as alcohol educators.

(c)   Take action by educating their clients about alcohol.

(d)   Be able to use and apply their previous experience, training and knowledge to alcohol education.

(e)   Be able to see the needs of the whole person in relation to their life situation and identify the way alcohol fits into this picture.

27

(f)   Be able to apply educational strategies to alcohol problems at primary, secondary and tertiary levels of prevention.

(g)   Have knowledge about the development of an individual's drinking behaviour and how it is influenced by social, legal, cultural, economic, psychological and genetic factors.

(h)   Have knowledge of the influence on drinking patterns in our society of cultural, economic, fiscal, legal and educational factors.

(i)   Have knowledge about the biochemical and pharmacological properties of alcohol and its part in the host-agent-environment system.

(j)   Be aware of, and understand, current theories about alcohol use and abuse.

The aims seemed highly unrealistic, given the amount of time we had. A diagram within the manual helped, though, by breaking this down into knowledge, attitudes and skills. I was beginning at this stage to wonder if I had enough knowledge to enable me to devote sufficent time to explore my attitudes and skills.

6.   **Working through the manual - small sub-groupings planning and presenting the exercises**

These sessions, where small sub-groups went off to plan and present the exercises contained in the manual, formed the bulk of the key tutors' course. Individuals were elected to work in small groups and were encouraged to involve each member of the small group in the presentation. During these presentations the rest of the course members were used as trainees. Unfortunately, these small groups were not without considerable tension. This arose because each group contained within it individual participants with a range of knowledge, experience and training expertise. This meant that at times group members found it difficult to reach agreement as to how sessions should be planned and presented. One advantage of this structure was that it gave members insight into the difficulties most groups experience in trying to reach a consensus. It did not, however, necessarily afford greater awareness as to how they, themselves, might go about planning a training session, using the DCM material given. It is important to note that an understanding of group dynamics is essential to using participatory exercises but, given the limited amount of time

28

available, it might have been worthwhile to have given space for individuals to work alone, both on planning and presenting material. This might have necessitated the tutors working separately, with only half of the group at any one time.

7.   The group presentations

These were very useful.   The benefits were two-fold, in that presenters acquired some experience of using the material, and received feedback on their presentation (training) skills.   At the same time, it was possible as a course member, to participate in a large number of other small group presentations.   This enabled one to experience the exercises from a participant's stand-point.   This model also gave people the opportunity to see a variety of interpretations given to the material contained within the DCM.

The above process was repeated three times in all, with individuals working within a variety of different sub-groupings.   This meant that people became thoroughly immersed in the DCM material, but there was a tendency for it to become rather repetitive.   The introduction of other activities, in between these presentations, might have alleviated this.   For example, the opportunity for viewing the training resources materials that the tutors had brought with them.

8.   Review sessions

Review sessions happened regularly throughout the course.   They occurred at natural breaks, when individuals had finished a specific section of the course.   This enabled tutors and participants to reflect upon how the course was going, to what extent it was meeting its objectives.   These 'objectives' were specifically the 'wants' identified by the participants on the first day.   There was a final review session at the end of the course.   From the feedback given to the tutors it was clear that the participants had gained a great deal from the course, and had found it a very useful and worthwhile experience.   People had especially valued the opportunity to re-examine their attitudes regarding alcohol use and to try out the exercises contained within the manual.

9.   The second part of the course 25-26 February 1986

The time between the first and second part of the course was three weeks.   Course members had been asked to do an interim task which involved some research into the local alcohol situation, either regarding local statistics or facilities etc.   The first part of the course involved some introductory exercises, which focused upon individuals' experiences and thoughts regarding alcohol use and abuse during the intervening weeks. People were then given the chance to share their findings from the interim task. After this, participants were again asked to specify what in particular they wanted to get out of this, the second half of the course. We were reminded of the 'wants' we had outlined in part one, and a few individuals volunteered additions to these. There was, however, a sense that much of the work had already been completed in the first half of the course. Participants seemed to want guidance as to what they might gain from this second part. What was on offer was an opportunity to examine the resources available, that is those which could be used on alcohol education programmes.

10. Review of the resources

Most of the afternoon was spent reviewing the resources. The tutors had amassed numerous books, articles, handbooks, videos etc on alcohol education. We were invited to familiarise ourselves with these, so that we might assess those which could be of benefit to us. This could have been a very useful session, but individuals seemed overwhelmed by choice, and tended to stay together, working the videos, rather than branch out to do their own individual research.

11. Using the Drinking Choices Manual

On the evening of the first day, participants were given another chance to delve into the DCM, in order to try out being slightly more innovative with the exercises. I experienced this session as useful because it gave me the opportunity to develop an exercise in greater depth. Many other participants, however, found the timing rather than the task difficult. It was hard to get back into the DCM after the break and following dinner!

12. Setting objectives

The second day started with an introductory exercise, and was followed by an input by one of the tutors on the role of prevention within alcohol education. After this we were given a 'model' to help us sort out our individual objectives with respect to any future training events we might be running. This made us concentrate on what specific type of events we could run, when we would run them, with whom and where. Having completed this individually, we were then divided along geographical lines so as to facilitate collective decision making with people in the same region. This proved to be very helpful, because it allowed individuals to clarify what it was they wanted to do following the course, and what they would have to put into action in order for this to occur. At the same time, having been identified along geographical lines meant that there was the beginning of a network. People started sharing addresses and telephone numbers, and arranging follow-up meetings.

13.   Course review

The afternoon was spent in reviewing the course overall, and participants filled in evaluation questionnaires, and gave feedback to the tutors. The final exercise allowed the group to appreciate each other, and their contribution to the course. It was a very nice ending, and everyone left feeling they had achieved a great deal. Specifically, they had worked through the DCM, experienced group planning, had received some feedback on their presentations and skills and experienced a series of exercises as a participant. They now knew about a range of materials they could use and had set down some obejctives for the future. At the same time, they had become part of a network of people who could offer support to each other and might be able to work together on some 'Drinking Choices' courses.

Reflections on the course

On reflection there were some extremely positive things about the experience:

1.   The location was excellent and it accommodated to the course requirements.

2.   The trainers 'modelled' the participative style. They were clear about the boundary of their role and structured the course well. Participants certainly took responsibility for their own learning.

3.   The course was well paced, with a balance of input, exercises and review.

4.   There was an abundance of information on alcohol education.

5.   Participants were enabled to work through and become familiar with the manual. This meant that people felt quite comfortable with the manual, and confident in their use of it.

My reservations are as follows:

1. Selection

The selection of participants seemed arbitrary. Many individuals seemed unclear about what they were embarking upon at the beginning of the course. Some, however, were quite clear that they would not be able to do much training upon completion of the course. The reasons given were lack of time, already having a very busy schedule, and not having the authority to initiate training of this kind in their organisation.

The participants came from a variety of backgrounds, had varying degrees of experience of alcohol education and differing theoretical perspectives. This aided, rather than took away from the course, except where an individual had recently been through a treatment programme. When individuals adhere to an 'abstinence' model, the model presented by the DCM is likely to be in conflict with their own. Such individuals could find the course rather threatening, both to themselves and to their sobriety.

Occasionally, it might be beneficial to work with people from the same agency: that is to get the agreement of the 'managers'/'policy-makers' to run an in-house course for staff involved in training (eg a Social Services Department). Those staff would then be assured of support for running further courses.

2. The 'cascade' model of training

The 'cascade' model of training, that is one individual passing their knowledge on to other trainees who then train a further group, is often better in theory than in practice. Its major drawback is that the information, skills and knowledge transmitted along the chain can end up becoming sadly depleted. The course aimed to explore individuals' attitudes, knowledge and skills, and whereas the DCM provides a constant reminder of the knowledge, it is easier to forget information related to attitudes and skills. This might be remedied if the course focused more upon working with and challenging individual attitudes, and providing more in-depth feedback on participants' skills as communicators and trainers in the participative mode.

3. Theoretical context of Drinking Choices

Given the numerous debates taking place within the drinking field, greater time could have been spent putting the key tutor course into context. Participants came from a variety of work settings, and had various degrees of knowledge and experience of alcohol use and abuse. Although many understood and agreed with the basic tenets behind the <u>Drinking Choices/Understanding Alcohol</u> programme, some individuals were struggling to come to terms with the underlying philosophy. If the course aims to explore attitudes, greater time needs to be given to debate these important issues. The present model, with its focus on planning and presentation, allows insufficient time for reflection and discussion. Participants are so concerned to understand, plan and deliver their presentations that major disagreements regarding beliefs are not dealt with. This created frustrations which were not resolved. One way these frustrations were handled was by people electing not to work with certain other participants. In essence, the <u>task</u> of the course became the planning and presentation of exercises rather than exercises providing a stimulus for a discussion of the issues involved in holding certain attitudes. I would suggest therefore that more time be devoted to discussing any conflicts, particularly at the end of individual sub-group presentations. This would enable people to talk through their difficulties, thus helping move them towards a re-evaluation of their attitudes.

4.   <u>Course design and structure</u>

Given the comments above, I feel that the course structure could be modified slightly in order to give people greater opportunity to understand the purpose of the course, and the expectation upon them, following its completion. I think the course design should incorporate an introductory day and would look as follows:

Introductory day

Four week gap

Three-day residential

Four week gap

Two-day residential

Key individuals could be invited to attend the 'Drinking Choices' course. They would attend the introductory day, at which the aims, objectives and style of the course could be made clear. They would be informed about any expectations upon them following the course. In addition, prospective participants would have the opportunity of getting to meet the tutors and their fellow group members. The <u>Drinking Choices Manual</u> could be introduced at this stage, and those members who still felt willing or able to continue with the course could take their manual away with them.

The three-day residential could follow the lines of the outline above, but with greater attention being paid to developing peoples' skills in planning and presentation. Course members could have detailed feedback on their skills with perhaps a video being available as an additional form of feedback. More time should be allowed for discussing any issues or disagreements which emerge. The tutors could take more opportunity to highlight the facilitation of certain group dynamics, such as conflict.

A month later the second two-day residential would take place, and this could focus on issues emerging since the first residential, as well as providing time for the exploration of what additional teaching resources exist. Some space could be made available for assessment of skills, and time to devise strategies for networking and running 'Drinking Choices' courses.

5. Pre-course information

Any literature sent to participants should spell out simply and clearly the philosophy of the course and its aims, objectives, and any expectations about participants prior, during and after they have completed the course. Clarity with respect to this information would allow people to select themselves out if they were unsuitable for the course.

6. Aims and objectives for the course

As I have already said, I feel that the aims of the course are too embracing. It is neither possible nor desirable to cover so much in so short a period of time. If participants were selected on the basis of having sufficient knowledge to feel comfortable with the material contained within the DCM, then it would be possible to concentrate on skills and attitudes. The feedback given on their skills should, therefore, give them the confidence to go on to run further courses.

7. The introduction of the Drinking Choices Manual

This manual can look intimidating on first viewing. Some would-be participants could be discouraged from attending a key tutors' course if they thought they would be expected to become familiar with so much, in so short a period of time. Busy professionals might think they would need to do a mass of additional 'homework', in order to become conversant with the material, and thus select themselves out.

If, however, the manual were introduced by the tutors, section by section, this might reduce the initial negative reaction. It is important that course members, or potential course members, be introduced to the manual sensitively, because it is in essence a very straightforward, well designed resource from which trainers can obtain useful, clear material.

8.   Style and content of the Drinking Choices Manual

I have no major criticism of the manual which I found simple and easy to work through. It contains an abundance of information for any trainee. One slight irritant is its tendency to see its 'client group' as predominantly white and male. There surely must be enough information about 'women and alcohol' to justify greater coverage, and people in other ethnic groupings must need educating about alcohol!

Conclusion

The Bristol course was designed to develop local networks of key tutors as outlined in the Action Plan of the South West alcohol education programme. It aimed to explore the knowledge, attitudes and skills needed by such alcohol educators. This is a rather daunting and perhaps unrealistic task given the time available. I believe that participants need to have a very thorough awareness of the various debates taking place within the alcohol field, prior to the course. The focus of the course could be, therefore, the opportunity for participants to examine their attitudes and develop their skills in participatory learning, within the 'Drinking Choices' framework.

Within this context, the role of the course tutors is paramount. They must be able to 'model' the skills involved in facilitating a participatory learning experience. In essence these skills are boundary keeping, negotiation, listening, clarifying and reflecting skills. They must present a clarity regarding:

(a)   aims, and objectives for the course;

(b)   the role of the course tutor and the limits to tutor responsibility;

(c)   the role of the participant, and the extent to which the participant is responsible for her/his own learning.

Essentially, the tutor structures the learning experience, in negotiation with the participant, but is not responsible for the learning of the participant.

For any participative course to succeed, there needs to be a shared understanding between tutor and participant regarding the nature of the course. There are various stages at which this understanding is achieved. These stages, in some sense, form a 'contract' between tutor and participant. The first stage involves any pre-course literature that is circulated regarding the course. The second occurs at the initial session of the course, and the third happens throughout, and at the end of the course, in the form of review sessions. Without clarity at any of these stages, it is difficult for participants to have a full understanding of the experience they are either about to have, or have just undergone.

Given the expectations placed upon individuals attending a 'Drinking Choices' key tutor course, it is important that they are given sufficient information and time prior to commencement to decide whether the course is suitable for them. With this in mind, I have outlined some changes to the administration, and structure of the course. I feel (a) there should be greater clarity regarding pre-course literature, and (b) there should be an introductory day, prior to the residential element, at which tutors meet with prospective members, to outline the course in detail, indicating the type of commitment required following the course. At the same time, I think there should be greater emphasis upon attitudes and skill development, and that participants should be able to demonstrate a certain level of knowledge of alcohol issues before being taken on to the course.

Note

1.   Barbara Howe in Chapter 5 indicates that an explanatory booklet on Drinking choices: a model for interdisciplinary action is used by many DC courses and does provide some of the pre-course information desired by the author.

3

PILOT SURVEY OF THE PARTICIPANTS OF 'DRINKING CHOICES' COURSES IN SOUTH WEST ENGLAND

Kevin Doogan

Introduction

As part of the programme of evaluation of the South West alcohol education programme conducted by the School for Advanced Urban Studies, a survey was carried out of the 'Drinking Choices' (DC) courses organised in Bristol, Falmouth, Exeter and Taunton. This piece of research tried to complement the mainly qualitative research methods[1] the research team had employed and it was also used to feed into the quantitative research carried out within the national programme of DC course evaluation.[2] It has been constructed as a pilot exercise in the hope that its findings will shape the design of any larger scale survey instruments.

As explained in Chapter 1 the Action Plan of the South West alcohol education programme stressed the need for a major training initiative for alcohol educators. The main mechanism for achieving this was to be the South Western Dissemination Programme for what is known as the Drinking Choices Manual,[3] developed by Ina Simnett, Linda Wright and Martin Evans for the HEC and TACADE. The dissemination has involved a series of residential key tutor training courses, the first five of which are covered by this report. The Action Plan defined key tutors as "people with existing training responsibilities in the field of health/alcohol education". These tutors would then run their own courses for local alcohol educators who would in turn run courses for clients "thus building a pyramidal structure". This report is principally concerned with an analysis of whether this 'pyramidal structure' has begun to develop in the South West because of these courses. It is not intended as an evaluation of the Drinking Choices Manual, which offers a much wider range of aims and objectives.

In the design of the survey the research team acknowledged that the study group was heterogeneous in character but also small in number and so it attempted to shape a set of questionnaires suitable to a group of respondents of greatly differing backgrounds and responsibilities and who would also differ in the roles and perspectives they would bring to bear on the alcohol education process. Consequently the research was ambitious in scope and also pursued specific lines of inquiry in its questioning. A further complication arose in the timing of this piece of research work. The team was placed in the most unusual situation of surveying people, seeking to elicit their expectations prior to participating on the course, after some of them had already taken part on the DC course. In short it asked people to try and remember what they were thinking and feeling prior to attending a course that would possibly have affected those same thoughts and feelings. Clearly this retrospective method might upset the purists among the research fraternity, and was indeed the cause of no small anxiety for the author, but the dictates of generating a study group out of a small population eventually silenced any objections, and lingering doubts were assuaged by the inclusion of a number of open-ended questions.

The survey

Prior to attending the course, on completing the course and six months after the course, the participants were asked to complete three questionnaires (see Appendix at end of this publication). The courses surveyed were as follows:

	Respondents to questionnaires	
	I & II	III
Falmouth October 1984	15	15
Taunton February 1985	15	15
Taunton May 1985	10	10
Exeter October 1985	6	6
Bristol February 1986	15	N/A
TOTAL	61	46

In total 61 people responded and this represents a response rate of 76% since 77 people had attended the five courses.

The study group proved to be a highly disparate group of people spread widely across the following occupations.

	No	%
Community or youth worker	3	4.9
Health education officer	8	13.1
Health visitor	1	1.6
Hospital doctor	2	3.3
Nurse or nurse tutor	3	4.9
Personnel or welfare officer	3	4.9
Probation	8	13.1
School teacher/head teacher	8	13.1
Social worker/manager/trainer	4	6.6
Voluntary counsellor	3	4.9
Self employed	2	3.3
Voluntary sector manager	8	13.1
Other	3	4.9
Road safety officer	1	1.6
General practitioner	1	1.6
Police officer	3	4.9
TOTAL	61	100%

However the course participants cluster around probation, school teacher, voluntary sector managers and health education officers who account for more than half of all respondents. Despite the variety of posts held by course participants, the group as a whole seem to hold positions with a substantial training responsibility since some 70% described their job thus in response to being asked this question.

Attitudes towards alcohol education

With regard to attitudes towards alcohol education and its objectives an attempt has been made to examine the assumptions that might have focused alcohol education on a specific client group or those that viewed its benefits applying to the wider community. It was found that 85% strongly felt that 'alcohol education is everyone's business' and some 90% felt strongly that alcohol education needed to help people to make informed choices about the use of alcohol. Most people also felt alcohol education could change drinking patterns. From these data it can be assumed that, prior to entering the course, the group believes that alcohol education is of general public concern and can effect changes in alcohol consumption. This indicates the positive frame of mind with which the participants enter the course and is also reflected in the self-confidence they expressed in their own abilities to be alcohol educators with 13% feeling 'very confident', and 67% 'fairly confident' about their own ability to be an alcohol educator.

Attitudes towards the 'Drinking Choices' course

When asked their views of the course they had attended, the responses must give satisfaction to the course organisers. Some 80% felt that the workload during the course was about right; the course was only occasionally stressful, 62% rated the group spirit and identity as being excellent or very good with a further 26% rating the course to have a good group spirit; the performance of team leaders scored highly with 70% saying they were 'excellent' or 'very good'; the scope of information was held to be 'excellent' or 'very good' by the majority; and similar results are offered for the presentation of materials. It is not surprising, therefore, that a substantial 87% felt their abilities as alcohol educators had been enhanced by attending the course.

The course rates well according to a number of indicators, as shown above, but there is still a need to clarify what it is in the course that is of greatest interest to the participant. The following table indicates the range of response:

What did you most want out of the 'Drinking Choices' course?

	No	%
More information on alcohol related issues	28	45.9
Confidence to apply participative learning techniques to alcohol education	12	19.7
Confidence to apply participative learning techniques to other topics	2	3.3
Confidence to run a full 'Drinking Choices' course	6	9.8
Confidence to use alcohol education as part of a client treatment programme	7	11.5
Confidence to present alcohol education talks	0	0.3
An opportunity to meet other people	2	3.3
Personal development	2	3.3
Other	2	3.3
TOTAL	61	100

Almost half the group came to the DC course primarily seeking more information on alcohol education. Only 10% entered seeking to acquire the skills to run a full 'Drinking Choices' course. However, almost 20% were mostly concerned with using participative learning techniques. From these and earlier responses it can be seen that course participants do not lack confidence to engage in alcohol education and consequently do not rate as important those developmental aspects of the course which seek to build up their self-esteem since it is already sufficient in their own minds. Primary concerns are the acquisition of information of alcohol related issues since the greatest perceived need is to fill the information gap in this area. However a small but significant number are concerned with acquiring the specific skills to adapt participative learning techniques to their own work.

Outcomes of the course

As part of the later follow-up questionnaire sent to course participants in Taunton, Exeter and Falmouth, participants were asked if they had run or intended to run a full DC course since taking part in their own course.

	Yes %	No %	Don't know %
Have you run a full DC course?	9	91	
Do you intend to run a full DC course?	35	63	2

Only four people from the South West region indicated they had run full DC courses, although there were early ambitions to do so registered by a further 16 people. However the large majority of the study group never had any intentions of running full 'Drinking Choices' courses. Both these figures are understandable if related to the sets of interests expressed by the participants, on entering the course, which demonstrate that only a small minority wish to become key tutors.

However, with regard to the minority who might have wished to organise a full DC course, but whose ambitions were not realised, the questionnaire inquired into the reasons preventing initiatives of this kind. For the large part two reasons feature in the responses. Firstly a lack of resources is offered by more than one third of respondents and a similar proportion find that a full 'Drinking Choices' course was inappropriate to their own work and their organisation.

To summarise the data so far we find the following:

1. The participants feel alcohol education is everyone's responsibility.

2. The courses were very good, with excellent group spirit, reasonably good scope of information and team leaders etc.

3. Most participants did have a major training responsibility in their posts.

4. They largely felt that alcohol education could affect drinking patterns.

5. They felt confident in themselves as alcohol educators and also felt that their skills had been improved by the course.

However,

6. Very few people had organised DC courses.

7. The large majority never had any intention of organising further full six day courses themselves.

8. For the minority who had intentions in this direction the obstacles were institutional and not individual.

If the 'cascade' model depends on key tutors going on to run their own full courses, then the fact that most people have no intention of running such courses begs closer scrutiny. The responses to two open-ended questions begin to throw light on the processes at work. The questionnaire asked about the ways participants were recruited to the course and asked them to elaborate on their interests in attending.

When asked how they heard of the course the following responses show a great variety of sources:

> The Director of the Somerset Council on Alcoholism suggested same and encouraged my attending.

> Really can't remember. It would be either through Libra or Health Visitors' Memo from Health Education Department County Hall.

> Through Devon Council on Alcoholism.

> Circular to HMP Dartmoor.

> As soon as I commenced my present post (November '84) I contacted the Regional Co-ordinator to learn about the SW Programme and so learned about DC.

> From NE England Alcohol Education Project.

> Via Principal Training Officer SSD.

> Via Senior Assistant, Mental Health Service, Somerset SSD.

> Through Health Education Unit, Dorchester.

Through HEO at Torbay Health Authority.

Through the Director of the Somerset Council on Alcoholism.

Approached by Head who received a letter from LEA.

Through the Prison Training Programme.

Via the North Devon Council for Alcoholism.

Local health education officer.

Via Somerset Council on Alcoholism.

Details were sent to our office via our headquarters.

Advertising for the course.

From South Devon HEO.

Local Health Education Unit.

Via my own department and health service colleagues.

Received letter asking if someone could attend.

Through HEC mailing for South West programme.

Went on National Dissemination advertised through HEC.

Prison Circular when attached to Probation Department.

From senior probation officer.

A visit from the Regional Co-ordinator.

Mailing through South West HEC.

Probation HQ.

By being a member of Regional Advisory Committee of the South West alcohol education programme.

Cornwall Health Education Unit Personnel.

At a day conference.

From the Regional Co-ordinator.

These responses suggest a variety of sources of information, formal and informal, and there is possibly a suggestion of a degree of arbitrariness[4] to the way in which people were selected to take part in the course. This is corroborated in the answers given by two people on the Taunton course when asked to offer further comments on the course. One said:

> Probably my own fault! but the content of the course and the fact that it was hoped to turn the participants into Alcohol Educators was not what I envisaged. I think that more pre-course information should be more carefully selected ie for those who are keen to teach groups.

And another from the same course offered this view:

> I feel that many of us were on the wrong course. We should have been on a course giving us information about alcohol, not being trained to be tutors. A lot of time spent allowing us time to practise teaching could have been spent gaining more information.

A Falmouth participant suggested:

> Too many communication exercises, not enough real alcohol education.

Again from Falmouth:

> A good working knowledge of alcohol was assumed by course leaders - mine is not that good.

However, not all views expressed were in this vein. From Falmouth again came this response:

> I would have preferred 'the opportunity' to work through the whole manual in a tutor's role rather than just one section of it. I felt that I had experienced the learner/group member role to a much greater extent than that of a tutor. I would have enjoyed the luxury of experimenting as a tutor with more of the content.

It can be seen from these comments that there are two, probably related, sets of responses. On the one hand it appears that some of the recruitment of the course has been conducted in an ad hoc manner and also, perhaps as a consequence, course members do not fit the mould of trainee key tutors. Course members make a distinction between continuing and developing their alcohol education activities and becoming a 'key tutor'. The obvious need for alcohol information - 'real alcohol education' - expressed by many attending the early courses suggests a mismatch between the target audience and the actual audience. This gap may well have narrowed in later courses but it is an observable phenomenon in the early days of the DC courses.

Notwithstanding this, people do feel the need to attend and have their own requirements to be satisfied by the DC course. When asked to describe the follow-up support necessary to function as alcohol educators course members are quite explicit in stating their requirements, as can be seen from the following nine examples:

1. County based meetings of key tutors from all courses. Newsletter.

2. Regular workshops.

3. A network of contacts.

4. I have found that over the last 12 months I have lost the confidence. I felt that a three month reunion would be valid.

5. More regular meetings of other people who have done the course, not the whole group, but four or five people who are in/near your district.

6. Regular information and update of resources - widespread availability of above.

7. To be an alcohol educator as a prison officer in many respects is very limited due to detailed jobs and shifts etc. It would have to be a specified job to be a success. This type of work does not come under a prison task list.

8. Updated refresher course on a district basis.

9. Need Regional Organiser (HEC) to support a network of support and communication.

There is evidently a demand for a sympathetic support network, probably locally based as well as the perceived need for the South West programme to provide more of a co-ordination role in the region. However that sense of isolation and the associated lack of motivation and confidence to organise future alcohol education activities has in fact been overcome in certain localities. This is demonstrated by the answers to the question asking whether a local DC support network had developed locally:

	No	%
Yes	26	56.5
No	13	28.3
Don't know	6	13.0
No response	1	2.2
TOTAL	46	100

This table would appear to show a high number of people enjoying the support of local networks. These networks could provide a useful focus for further research.

Other alcohol education activities

The fact that most participants did not go on to run full six day courses does not mean that the majority had not been involved in alcohol education since their course. 10 participants were unable to provide some mention of any such activities in response to the open ended question on this subject. The level and volume of activity for the other 36 was very varied as can be seen in the Appendix at the end of this chapter which lists all the replies received to this question.

Specific groups of participants

Up until now the views and responses of the whole study group have been described without regard to specific interests within it. This is hardly surprising in view of the small population and the weak base from which any sub group characteristics are based. However, the author did feel an obligation to re-classify the responses according to two criteria. In the first instance he looked at the sets of responses from each course and examined any divergence of opinions among different courses. With some relief broadly similar sets of responses were found to all questions, although the six month follow-up for the Bristol course is yet to be completed, and so it is possible to feel a small degree of confidence that, although our findings are based on a small number of responses, the responses are not wholly untypical or unrepresentative of the experience of those taking part in the early courses.

In the second case, an examination was made of the occupations of course members and these were re-classified according to whether the core of the role seemed to be geared to the primary, secondary or tertiary levels of prevention. Tertiary represents intervention directed at a particular client, secondary represents an intervention with an 'at risk' population, and primary offers general information to the whole community. It was the considered opinion of the research team that the following occupations might be grouped thus, although it is appreciated that others may wish to challenge the logic or the fairness of the allocation.

Occupation	Level of prevention
Community worker, youth worker	Secondary
General practitioner	Tertiary
Health education officer	Primary
Health visitor	Secondary
Hospital doctor	Tertiary
Nurse/nurse tutor	Tertiary
Personnel/welfare officer	Secondary
Police officer	Tertiary
Probation	Tertiary
School teacher/head teacher	Primary
Social worker/manager/trainer	Secondary
Voluntary counsellor	Secondary
Self employed	Secondary
Voluntary sector manager	Secondary
Road safety officer	Secondary
Other	Other

When data is collected from these responses of primary, secondary and tertiary groups, there are interesting similarities and differences of opinion offered. Perhaps most significant is the fact that all three groups expect to gain, and have gained, most from the course in terms of the information they receive, and judge the usefulness of the course primarily in terms of acquiring knowledge of alcohol related issues. Furthermore they all seem to be similarly disinclined to run full DC courses in the future. This was surprising since one might have assumed that the primary group should be concerned with the dissemination of general information in the wider community.

The differences between the groups are shown in such factors as the training responsibilities they carry in their job with 94% of the primary group having a major training responsibility, 74% of the secondary group and 58% of the tertiary group. Also of interest is the slight difference in views between these three sets of people in their attitudes towards the balance of people on the courses with the primary recording the higher satisfaction while secondary and tertiary groups felt that psychiatric, other medical fields, and social services were all under-represented amongst course members.

Conclusion

Any concluding remarks must be made with some qualification about the small size of our study group and the heterogeneous nature of the population, both of which demand that comments are illustrative rather than definitive. There is also some security derived from the fact that any significant errors of interpretation should be counter-balanced by the qualitative evaluation carried out by the research team.

As is customary in drawing conclusions from evaluation, a useful distinction can be made between process-based evaluation and product-based evaluation. In studying process one looks at course content, participation, recruitment and other organisational aspects. Product-based evaluation on the other hand concerns itself with outcomes, the attainment of objectives as well as attempting to explain unfulfilled ambition.

In focusing on the processes at work in the DC courses, the findings demonstrate that, from the perspective of the participants, the courses manage to notch up certain successes. They provide the desired information on alcohol related issues and use much favoured techniques with participative learning, particularly popular amongst course members. Participants generally rate the group spirit, the performance of team leaders and the teaching materials used as excellent or very good. The mixed group of people attending the course is seen as a strength although the medical profession may be insufficiently represented in some groups. Given the fact that almost all repondents considered alcohol education to be of general importance to the community and that most people have a major training responsibility then the perceived enhancement of their skills as alcohol educators must rate as a success for the course and give some satisfaction to the course organisers.

However, a less satisfactory picture emerges with regard to whether the output from these training courses indicates the development of a 'pyramidal structure'. If the 'cascade' model is used and the assumption operates that key tutor courses should have a catalytic effect spanning a wider number of key tutor groups in some self replicating fashion, then clearly one must acknowledge the obstacles to this self expanding model. The survey identified two sets of obstacles:

1. Institutional eg lack of resources; an incompatability between their own alcohol education activities and running DC courses etc.

2. Individual eg lack of confidence, motivation, abilities etc.

The results clearly point to the constraints of the institution for most participants and the view that organising full DC courses does not fit easily with their own alcohol education activities. The author has attempted to examine the institutional environment by grouping the respondents into primary, secondary and tertiary layers of intervention. It was found that in the primary group the appropriateness of the 'cascade' model to their role is most noticeable whilst secondary and tertiary groups are held back more noticeably by lack of time and resources.

If the 'cascade' model is maintained there is an observable mismatch between the target population and the actual population attending the courses. There are certain possible issues arising from this gap:

1. That recruitment practices might be changed so as to clarify both the course objectives and expectations about future key tutor activities. This solution essentially involves changing the audience for the course.

2. The course syllabus might be altered to focus more activities on developing strategies that overcome institutional constraints. This might involve training in negotiation skills, the sharing of experiences in overcoming institutional obstacles and developing good practice in establishing supportive networks etc. This solution therefore implies a

change of the course content but assumes maintenance of the original objectives.

3.   The other solution lies in a curriculum modification changing the course to enable the development of alcohol education activities that are specific and appropriate to the role and responsibility of each participant.   This could entail some redefinition of the key tutor concept and also the abandonment of the 'cascade' model.   This solution implies a significant change in both objectives and in course content.

It is obviously for others to determine which option is adopted.   If judged from no other perspective than that of the course participants the early indications point both to a reassessment of the means and also more significantly to the ends.

References

1.   An outline of the main components of the research is provided in **Harrison, L. and Means, R.** (1986) 'Implementing an holistic approach to alcohol education', Health Education Journal, Vol 45, No 3, pp 132-136.

2.   See Chapter 5 by Barbara Howe for a presentation of some of the national data.

3.   **Simnett, I., Wright, L. and Evans, M.** (1982) Drinking Choices: a training manual for alcohol educators, TACADE/HEC.

4.   See Chapter 1 by Lyn Harrison and Robin Means for a discussion of the main recruitment channels used by the Regional Co-ordinator and Deputy Co-ordinator for the early courses.

APPENDIX to Chapter 3

Answers to open ended questions on alcohol education activities carried out since course

1. Several one-day sessions/workshops run in conjunction with a fellow key tutor (police officer/prison officer).

2. Material used in manual in general alcohol education sessions. These sessions are a normal part of his work responsibilities (voluntary sector manager).

3. Four full courses that have trained 62 people. Several other short courses, workshops etc. Alcohol education is part of his work responsibilities (voluntary sector manager).

4. Run discussion group on occasions about alcohol education for prisoners (police officer/prison officer).

5. DCM used as preparation for the commencement of an alcohol education programme run jointly by the Council on Alcoholism and the Probation Service. Each course contains eight consecutive sessions of two hours each. The first one started on 14 January and they are still continuing (probation).

6. Helped to run a study day on 'Understanding Alcohol' (voluntary sector manager).

7. Nothing listed (voluntary counsellor).

8. Two-day workshop on alcohol education was run on an interagency basis. He also arranged a study day for the Probation Service (probation).

9. A stimulus to a wide range of activities including setting up briefing conference, forming local alcohol forums, study days and workshops. With regard to the last two, she had helped to run a weekend course for youth leaders and a presentation

to the Safety Committee of Mendip District Council (health education officer).

10. This individual has run two day only workshops in conjunction with a fellow key tutor. She has used material and approach of DCM in her health education work in secondary schools. This involves 400 pupils in groups of 17-24 (school teacher/head teacher).

11. This FE college teacher has run various in-service training events for other teaching staff. Some sessions have also been arranged for students as part of their courses (personnel/welfare officer).

12. Nothing listed (hospital doctor).

13. Since course, he has continued to be involved with a local alcohol abuse forum. He has used manual in discussions with his staff (social worker/manager/trainer).

14. Involved in an alcohol support group (voluntary counsellor).

15. She has not organised any groups but she has continued to be involved with Libra groups (voluntary counsellor).

16. She has since run various sessions in local schools and colleges (voluntary sector manager).

17. Three sessions have been run for prison staff. He has also put in an input at regional management level (community worker/youth worker).

18. This tutor has not run specific events but DCM stimulated her to try much harder to place alcohol education higher on the agenda of a variety of agencies. She expects this to reap dividends (health education officer).

19. Nothing listed (health education officer).

20. Involved in several alcohol related activities including a monthly study session (social worker/manager/trainer).

21. None except work with individual clients (about four in number) (social worker/manager/trainer).

22. He has participated in two one-day workshops. He has given talks to the local college of further education. He has run a half-day seminar with local community nurses (nurse/nurse tutor).

23. He has helped to set up a community based project through the Community College (community worker/youth worker).

24. Given a paper at an inter-agency meeting of professionals (general practitioner).

25. Eight half-day sessions (for professionals?) run in a market town, one in another and further are planned. Material from DCM has been integrated into a variety of activities including nine one-day courses for voluntary counsellors (voluntary sector manager).

26. She uses some material from DCM in her personal, social and moral education courses for fourth and fifth years. DCM material also used in in-service training/advice for colleagues (school teacher/head teacher).

27. Nothing listed (police officer/prison officer).

28. Nothing listed (health education officer).

29. This tutor has been involved in development of a scheme to raise interest and awareness in the hospital. This has included the introduction of alcohol education as a specific part of the new nurse training curriculum (nurse/nurse tutor).

30. Nothing listed (probation).

31. Has run two alcohol training days for probation teams with another key tutor. All probation teams have now been offered this course. They tried to set up an alcohol education programme for probation clients but there were no attenders (probation).

32. Helped to argue the case for a research post to investigate importance of alcohol in a variety of crimes. He has run two alcohol training courses for probation teams. They tried to set up an alcohol education programme for probation clients but there were no attenders (probation).

33. Industrial action has stopped this teacher developing sessions (school teacher/head teacher).

34. Used material from DCM in a variety of courses, study days but this individual lives and works outside the South West (voluntary sector manager).

35. Involved in a study day on alcohol education (social worker/manager/trainer).

36. Plans to present alcohol education and training module to college students and staff in the next term (school teacher/head teacher/education lecturer).

37. None listed (nurse/nurse tutor).

38. None listed (health education officer).

39. Worked in school as part of the programme's research into the use of videos by teachers (school teacher trainer).

40. Nothing specifically due to course (voluntary sector educator).

41. Has provided an information and advice centre as well as giving seminars and talks. Liaised with naval psychiatric services (personnel/welfare officer).

42. More informative with friends (self-employed).

43. Hopes to become part of work-based team providing alcohol education (personnel/welfare officer).

44. Briefed headquarters and training officers: allocated training time with probation officers. Identified alcohol liaison officers to attend training sessions for probation officers and commence client alcohol education groups in autumn. Investigating using course learning to work with drinking drivers as alternative to custody (probation).

45. None (education lecturer).

46. Organised evening session at youth club (cancelled due to lack of interest (community/youth worker).

4

THE DEVELOPMENT OF KEY TUTOR 'DRINKING CHOICES' COURSES IN SOUTH WEST ENGLAND

Derek Close

Introduction

The Action Plan for the South West Understanding Alcohol programme called for the training of key tutors throughout the region based on the Drinking Choices Manual (DCM). The DCM had developed out of that part of the HEC's Tyne Tees Alcohol Campaign that ran from 1974 to 1982. It was seen as a tool with which professionals engaged in alcohol education could develop their knowledge base about alcohol, as well as their attitudes and skills as alcohol educators.

As described in previous chapters, the manual listed 10 objectives for participants on completion of the course. These ranged from participants holding the attitude that education can be an effective means of prevention to participants being able to apply educational strategies to alcohol problems at primary, secondary and tertiary levels of prevention.

The DCM describes the course approach as using a participatory group work approach, focusing on learning rather than teaching. For those unfamiliar with this approach the manual offers a brief introduction to these techniques.

Using the DCM as a basic resource it was intended that a network of key tutors would be trained throughout the South West region. The model put forward in the Action Plan saw the key tutors training alcohol educators who would in turn educate their 'clients' about alcohol. The plan stressed that key tutors would be people with a training responsibility within the field of health/alcohol education. The 'Drinking Choices' courses were seen as inter-disciplinary and it was intended that key tutors would then work with their own professional colleagues training them as alcohol educators.

Recruitment information for key tutor 'Drinking Choices' (KTDC) courses in the South West stayed close to that outlined in the DCM although it was more specific in that it said that the role of the key tutors was to:

1. Run courses for people (health promoters, alcohol educators) within their agency whom they have identified as having a potential role in the programme.

2. Act as local catalysts for the development of local activities through supporting the health promoters/alcohol educators they train.

The criteria for selection were as follows:

1. They should be in a position to have the time and be free to run 'Drinking Choices' courses.

2. They should already have skills as trainers and in using group work approaches (or additional training in these skills should be made available to them, eg through the 'working with groups' course).

3. They should be interested in the broad field of education for life/life and social skills education/personal and social education/health promotion.

4. They should be interested in developing a role in the South West alcohol programme and understand that the approach of the programme is to promote sensible drinking through stimulating informed debate and encouraging people to make informed choices. The emphasis of the programme is on primary prevention, ie to help us all to identify actions which will prevent harm occurring related to alcohol.

5. They should be interested in working on an inter-disiplinary basis and in developing inter-agency responses.

It was intended that the Regional Co-ordinator and her deputy would maintain and support the key tutor network throughout the region and that there would be follow up courses four to six months after the original training. The pattern of courses that evolved was two to three courses a year consisting of an initial three day block followed four to six weeks later by another two/three day block. In the interim period participants were asked to work on some aspect of alcohol education or to research local patterns of drinking, costs, marketing etc.

The Taunton course

My involvement with the programme as a trainer began when I was invited to run the 'Drinking Choices' course scheduled for May/June 1985 at Taunton. This was due to the resignation of the Regional Co-ordinator who had already run two 'Drinking Choices' courses as tutor at Falmouth (October 1984), and at Taunton (January 1985). I came to the programme with experience of working with young people as a teacher and youth worker and as a trainer working with adults in staff and personal development using participatory groupwork techniques. I had very little knowledge of the alcohol field.

At this time I had the opportunity to take part in the follow up to the Falmouth course. It was obvious that the majority of the participants had enjoyed and appreciated the original training and that the course had helped develop knowledge and attitudes and to some extent, skills. What I did find though, was a lack of clarity as to what was meant by a primary prevention programme and several participants had as their main concern the treatment and counselling of problem drinkers. It was clear that they did not intend to implement the 'Drinking Choices' course in the way that had been originally intended and it appeared they were going to use the DCM as a traditional teaching tool. Many of the other participants, while sympathetic to the participatory group work approach, had found it difficult to organise a key tutor 'Drinking Choices' course, as they lacked sufficient authority within their organisation and had not received the support of their managers. To this extent it was felt that either the original recruiting, or the contracting, had not been precise enough.

My experience of the Taunton course confirmed these feelings. I felt that at a personal level the outcome for participants was a good one: they went away feeling positive about the programme and with enhanced personal and training skills enabling them to work in the alcohol education field. However, the majority of participants had little idea of what was expected of them from their organisations and were not at all clear as to how they could put their training as key tutors into practice. Their employers had no clear policy on alcohol education so these.key tutors were in the position of having to make up their own policy as best they could or of trying to influence their organisations to take some steps in that direction. This led to high levels of anxiety during the course, and presumably afterwards, for many of the participants. We also had to deal with the issue of what the programme was about in terms of primary prevention.

In one sense this did not matter, because as a newcomer with no control over the recruitment and very little alcohol knowledge I felt it important to work with the participants' concerns and issues as a way of demonstrating participatory experiential learning. We used the DCM as a basic resource enabling participants to experience some of the materials and to obtain feedback on their presentations. More importantly I felt, we spent time reviewing the experience and I encouraged the setting up of mutual support groups on both a professional and geographical basis. We also spent some time working on action plans.

Feedback from participants also identified the following issues:

1.   The problem of 'owning' the DCM material.

2.   The inappropriateness of some of the material, in particular that which relates to the Tyne Tees campaign.

3.   The need for more training in groupwork skills.

4.   The length of the course and getting 'time off'.

5.   Where future support would come from.

6.   Using the DCM material in a different way to that intended.

It was not possible at this point to develop the training to take account of this feedback and my own observations, as recruitment for the next course had already taken place and the national disseminator for the 'Drinking Choices' courses had been booked to tutor with me on the next two 'Drinking Choices' courses (October 1985 and February 1986). To complicate matters it was at this point that the Deputy Co-ordinator handed in her notice resulting in a hiatus in the organisation and co-ordination of the programme between September 1985 and March 1986.

The Exeter, North Devon and Bristol courses

The Exeter 'Drinking Choices' course was delivered using a model that was closer to that originally envisaged in the DCM. We did have three experienced trainers on this course and to a large extent we were unable to meet their needs, as the majority of the participants were again not trainers and were using the course to clarify their position in relation to alcohol education, as well as looking for information and skills that would enable them to operate more effectively as alcohol educators. Feedback also suggested that the course was too long and that the value of the interim tasks was limited.

In January 1986 I was invited by one of the original trained key tutors, a health education officer from North Devon, to put on a special three day KTDC course for 13 people from North Devon. This proved to be very successful and enabled the group to work with specific concerns and issues. When it came to action plans it was clear there was much value in working with a group from a clear geographical area and it offered the prospect of better mutual support.

The February 'Drinking Choices' course held in Bristol followed the traditional pattern, but with an innovation in terms of recruitment. District Co-ordinators from Frenchay and Bath were in post at this point and it was suggested to them that they not only attend the course themselves, but that they identified and recruited people in their locality, to attend the course. This group would then form the basis of a local training team. The two Co-ordinators responded positively to this suggestion, so two teams from Frenchay and Bath formed the basis of the Bristol course.

Amending the training strategy

As a result of these experiences and because of developments that were taking place within the programme itself it now became possible to make further proposals as to the development of training throughout the programme. It was recognised that in the same way that the programme was starting to develop and be devolved to local district level, it was necessary for the training element to develop in recognition of these changes.

On the whole the training of key tutors was working reasonably well, but there were indications that some key tutors were dropping out after the initial training and that others were finding it difficult to utilise their training in a constructive way. The reasons for this appeared to be:

1. The relevance and appropriateness of the original training.

2. Lack of support and stimulation at local level.

3. An inability to contract with employers to work in the area of alcohol education.

It also appeared that insufficient distinction was being made between key tutors and alcohol educators as was originally envisaged so that key tutors and alcohol educators were participants on the same course, which was leading to confused expectations and outcomes. To a large extent this lack of distinction had been encouraged by the development of the programme. As part of the message that 'alcohol is everybody's business', it was felt that alcohol education would be stimulated if anyone with an interest could receive some training and then go away and do what they could within their own particular sphere of influence. In response to this situation it was decided to make a clearer distinction between key tutors and alcohol educators. At the same time District Co-ordinators for alcohol education were being appointed in response to a decision that the programme should be locally orientated.

It was therefore agreed that from this point any training offered by the regional programme should be more specifically targeted and that it would develop towards meeting specific needs. The training programme would therefore:

1.   Offer training courses at the regional level.

2.   Support, through consultancy, those key tutors, alcohol educators and District Co-ordinators who wish to run and develop their courses and materials.

3.   Develop core courses and introduce new courses in the light of experience and need.

It was decided to offer four different types of course. These were:

1.   Key tutor courses

These courses were for those with a training responsibility in their job and those who have an opportunity to be involved in a training role, such as managers, in relation to their immediate team. The course would offer an intensive three days' training, based on the DCM and would have as its objectives:

(a)   To explore the philosophy behind the Understanding Alcohol programme.

(b)   To provide alcohol related information.

(c)   To provide opportunities to be involved in participative and experimental methods of training.

(d)   To enable participants to devise their own objectives and action plans.

2. Alcohol educator courses

These courses were for those who through their work, community or family involvement, wish to take a more active role in alcohol education. The three day course would enable participants to:

(a) Explore the way in which alcohol affects our lives.

(b) Obtain alcohol related information.

(c) Experience approaches to educating people about alcohol.

(d) Draw up personal and/or group strategies and action plans.

3. Special interest/introductory day workshops

These events would be aimed at specific groups and/or areas of alcohol education. Suggested areas were:

(a) Alcohol and young people.

(b) Police/prison services/forces.

(c) Working with women.

(d) Alcohol policies.

(e) Special skills.

(f) Drinking and driving.

(g) Developing materials/resources.

(h) Support groups.

4. Regional workshops

These would be for key tutors, alcohol educators, District Co-ordinators and others working in the alcohol education field. The workshops would be three day residential experiences that would enable participants to share good practice, to examine blockages, to develop particular skills and to be introduced to new areas of work. Suggestions include groupwork skills, counselling, assertiveness, organisational change, team building, work with particular client groups etc.

These proposals are forming the basis of the training programme through to March 1987. Between September 1986 and March 1987 there will be two 'Drinking Choices' courses each of three days' duration, a three day regional workshop in February 1987 and several one day workshops are being negotiated with District

Alcohol Co-ordinators and Education Authority representatives. At the moment there has been no demand for an alcohol educators' course and it may be that this is an unnecessary tier in the design as District Alcohol Co-ordinators increasingly take on an educational role and key tutors start to develop work with their colleagues.

As most of the District Co-ordinators are now in post an increasingly important aspect of the training role will be the establishment and maintenance of good working relationships with the Co-ordinators. A good example of this has been the advertising and recruitment for the current 'Drinking Choices' courses. Co-ordinators were sent course details and application forms and were invited to recruit likely participants from their areas, with the intention of forming a nucleus of a training team. To some extent the course will be able to concentrate on the needs of these potential teams and time will be given to enable the local groups to work out training strategies and action plans. At the time of writing, October 1986, teams from West Dorset, Torbay, Somerset and Cornwall have been recruited for the November 1986 course. A further development in relation to the February 1987 course has taken place, in that two District Co-ordinators from Bristol will be co-tutoring with the training consultant on the course.

The advertising for the current courses has also been more specific than that for previous courses in that emphasis has been placed on recruitment from the two programme priority areas of young people and alcohol and the workplace. In addition intending participants have been asked to make sure that they have sufficient time to devote to alcohol education/training, and that they clear this with their line manager. They have also been asked to indicate their agreement to a continued involvement in alcohol education after completing the KTDC course.

These developments in the design and delivery of the 'Drinking Choices' course and the introduction of the additional training opportunities will ensure that:

1. The training element of the programme relates more closely to the programme's priority areas.

2. District Co-ordinators have the opportunity to be directly involved in training, to develop their skills and to influence the development of the training element in the programme.

3. Key tutors have a built in support system and the opportunity for further training.

4. The 'Drinking Choices' course itself will relate much more closely to the needs of the participants and will offer participants the opportunity to explore different ways of using the DCM.

Conclusion

In reviewing the development of the training for the programme, the following points emerge:

1. Opportunities have been made available for professionals from a wide variety of disciplines to work together on alcohol education. These workers have been able to examine their own attitudes towards alcohol, improve their knowledge base and develop appropriate training skills.

2. As a result of this initial training, many of these workers have been able to work more effectively with their clients, students and colleagues within the field of alcohol education. In most cases the original training material has been adapted and incorporated with other material, to produce training/educational packages that are more appropriate for use with client groups.

3. Throughout the South West there is now a basic network of key tutors and in some areas core groups of trainers/educators working with District Co-ordinators. The districts will need to utilise this network if the benefits of the original training are to be realised.

4. It is now recognised that the original objectives of the KTDC were not realistic given the time scale of the training. The objectives are probably more appropriate for longer term training and development.

5. It is also true to say that up to this point in time the dissemination model as originally envisaged has not worked very well, with only a very few key tutors running a further KTDC course. What has been noticeable is that where two or three people from the same organisation have attended a KTDC course, there has been a much higher percentage of training taking place for staff colleagues.

6. There has been a blurring of distinction between key tutors and alcohol educators and it may be that this distinction created an unnecessary tier in the training model.

7. Recruitment for courses is now much tighter as a result of early experiences which showed that KTDC courses were not appropriate for everyone. The message that the programme is about primary prevention appears to be getting through.

8. One major difficulty for key tutors has been the lack of alcohol policies of most organisations and employers who send key tutors on the courses. The negative side of this has been that key tutors have been unable to put their skills and learning into practice through lack of suitable opportunities and resources within their organisations. The positive side, backed by other publicity from the campaign, has been that organisations are starting to take alcohol education more seriously as a result of having a key tutor asking questions and looking for opportunities to work in the alcohol area within the organisation.

9. Insufficient attention has been given to the process by which people learn through participating in an experiential group process. It is unrealistic to expect that course participants will automatically be qualified to operate experientially in groups after having experienced the KTDC course. More attention needs to be paid to this very important aspect of learning.

The next phase of the training element within the programme will need to build on the foundations laid by the KTDC courses. While the DCM will remain an important resource, it is probable that future training will depend on ensuring that initial training of professionals, induction schemes and in-service training, have a clearly defined alcohol education element within them. There needs also to be a better understanding of the learning processes, particularly participatory, experiential learning, together with the development of closer links with other agencies within the alcohol education field.

5

THE NATIONAL DISSEMINATION OF 'DRINKING CHOICES' COURSES AND THE DEVELOPMENT OF A NEW DRUG EDUCATION COURSE

Barbara Howe

Introduction

During the period 1974-1986, the Health Education Council (HEC) sponsored an alcohol education campaign in the North East of England. One of the main findings taken from an evaluation of the early phases of the campaign (which was aimed at both the general public and professional workers) was that professionals were in need of further training in alcohol education if they were going to capitalise on the opportunities for alcohol education which occurred in their day to day work.

In response to this training need, <u>Drinking Choices, A Training Manual for Alcohol Educators</u>[1] (DC) was written and developed in the North East. With its emphasis on participatory learning and its focus on the knowledge, attitudes and skills needed by alcohol educators, its popularity as a training course soared and other parts of the country began to take note. The HEC sponsored two DC training courses at national level in 1984, but it was clear that these two events could not hope to cover the training needs of England and Wales. After enthusiastic feedback from participants at the workshops a three year project was established in 1985 in the School of Education at the University of Durham. This was known as the HEC Addictions Project and the work remit included:

1. Dissemination of DC courses throughout England and Wales.

2. Identification and evaluation of existing drug education materials.

3. Preparation of new materials on drugs and solvents in line with DC principles.

4. Piloting, evaluation and rewriting of those materials.

5. Production of a training package on drugs and solvents aimed at professionals, who deal with adults rather than children.[2]

6. Dissemination of the drugs training package throughout England and Wales.

A full-time Research Fellow (the author) was appointed to carry out this work with a part-time Senior Research Assistant whose specific task was related to the development of the drug education materials. Part-time secretarial support was also provided.

Drinking Choices courses - national dissemination

The Addictions Project was explained in the HEC Liaison Newsletter (July, 1985) which goes to every Health Education Unit in the country. The availability of the Research Fellow to run DC courses was stressed. Requests for courses began to arrive with increasing rapidity and were answered largely on a 'first come,first served' basis. To date, full courses have been run in the following parts of the country:

NW/SW Durham	September 1985
Ashington	Sept/Oct 1985
Exeter	Oct/Nov 1985
Preston	Nov/Dec 1985
Hull	Nov1985/Jan 1986
Great Yarmouth	Dec 1985/Jan 1986
Durham	Jan/March 1986
Hammersmith	Jan/March 1986
Bristol	February 1986
Bangor	April/May 1986
NW/SW Durham	April/June 1986
Rochdale	June/July 1986
NW/SW Durham	June/July 1986
Sheffield	June/July 1986
Edinburgh (National Scottish course)	Oct/Nov 1986
London	Oct/Nov 1986

Winchester	Nov/Dec 1986
Preston (part of NWRHA Prevention Programme)	Dec 1986/Jan 1987
Mid Wales (National Welsh course)	Feb/March 1987

With one or two exceptions, the majority of requests for DC courses have come from district health education officers (DHEOs) who want to offer multi-disciplinary alcohol education and training courses to professionals in their districts.

At first contact, the concept of a key tutor course is explained especially for those districts which want best 'value for money' from their one course. Key tutors are described as people with an explicit commitment to alcohol education in their day to day work who will, after DC training, undertake to run further DC courses for other groups of participants. Key tutors are an integral part of the pyramid or 'cascade' model of prevention, and are expected to pass on their knowledge and skills in alcohol education to other professionals who have some role in alcohol education such as nurses, probation officers, social workers, youth and community workers. The responsibility for course recruitment rests with the DHEO (or other) who has requested the course, although the project provides guidelines on advertising the course, materials/equipment needed, evaluation process, and follow-up sessions. The explanatory booklet <u>Drinking Choices. A model for interdisciplinary action</u> is used during the recruiting procedure.

Evaluation

Until April 1985, all DC courses were evaluated by means of a questionnaire completed by the participants at the end of their particular course. The questionnaire helped to assess changes made in knowledge, attitudes and skills in alcohol education and the resuts were collated by hand and an analysis forwarded to the DHEO (or other) who had originally convened the course.

This method of evaluation became less and less satisfactory in view of the mounting number of courses run at national level and, following consultation with staff at the School for Advanced Urban Studies (SAUS), Bristol University, a new method of evaluation was adopted. SAUS staff had devised a series of three questionnaires to evaluate the impact of key tutor DC courses run as part of the South West alcohol programme. With prior permission, the

Addictions Project adopted them for use with the national programme of dissemination for 'Drinking Choices'. The three questionnaires are used as follows:

Questionnaire I - to be completed by participants before attending a DC course to assess course expectations, degree of development of plans for alcohol education etc.

Questionnaire II - to be completed immediately after a DC course to assess its impact, future plans for alcohol education etc.

Questionnaire III - to be sent out twice yearly (for one year only) to assess follow-up of DC courses, establishment of support networks etc.

Statistical information in this chapter is taken from a computer analysis of data provided by Questionnaires I and II used on six DC courses run at national level (NW/SW Durham, Newham, Bangor, Rochdale, Sheffield, and NW/SW Durham). As Questionnaire III has yet to be mailed out to follow up the outcome of these courses, there is no information available on more long-term developments at present.

National findings - comparison with the South West

From the six DC courses detailed above, information was collected on Questionnaire I from a total of 96 participants and on Questionnaire II from 85 participants. The lesser number of returns for Questionnaire II is not necessarily an accurate indication of course drop-out rate as some people ask to leave the latter part of the course early (due to other work commitments) and are asked to complete and forward their questionnaire by post. In these circumstances, it is not uncommon for questionnaires not to arrive, hence the difference in the number of respondents to Questionnaires I and II.

One of the first major statistical differences to emerge from the national data relates to the occupations of the course participants with the majority coming from the NHS (67%) and the remainder mostly from the voluntary sector (17%) and local authorities (11%). This is perhaps not surprising given the vehicles used to advertise the DC courses such as the HEC Liaison Newsletter, Alcohol Concern's Journal and district health education newsletters which are circulated mainly among health service and/or voluntary sector workers. Participants cluster specifically around the following groups:

	%
School nursing sisters	29.1
Health visitors	10.4
Voluntary counsellors	8.3
Probation officers	6.25
Health education promotionofficers	5.2
Community psychiatric nurses	5.2
Youth and community workers	4.1
Volunteer workers	4.1

Although it is strongly recommended that DC courses are run on a multidisciplinary basis, two of the courses from which this data was taken were virtually single discipline courses. The event in North West/South West Durham had 28 school nursing sisters. At the Sheffield course, eight out of 11 participants worked for the Sheffield Alcohol Advisory Service on a voluntary basis as counsellors/befrienders.

Commitment to alcohol education

Questionnaire I attempts to assess commitment to alcohol education in terms of both the individual and his/her personal attitudes and the degree to which plans for future alcohol activities have been developed within his/her organisation before attendance on the DC course.

Out of a total of 96 respondents, 51% felt that their jobs included a major training responsibility, whilst 48% felt that they did not. Two people failed to answer the question at all. It is evident from the responses that key tutor courses (in the purest sense) are not taking place and that people attend DC courses for reasons (to be elucidated later) other than becoming trained key tutors.

70

1.   Individual commitment to alcohol education

Although the DC course does seem responsible for initiating some changes in the degree of personal commitment to alcohol education, the majority of participants believe that alcohol education can benefit most drinkers and that it can change the drinking patterns of the general population before they attend a DC course.   These beliefs appear to be reinforced by the DC experience as can be seen from Table 5.

Table 5:   The impact of the course upon the attitude of participants towards alcohol education

Q.   "Who can benefit most from alcohol education?"

		Responses	
		Before the course	After the course
1.	People with severe drinking problems	5%	1%
2.	Most people who drink	90%	98%
3.	Do not know	4%	1%

Q.   "Do you believe that alcohol education can change the drinking patterns of the general population?"

		Responses	
		Before the course	After the course
1.	Yes	56%	72%
2.	No	25%	4%
3.	Do not know	17%	24%

2. Organisations' commitment to alcohol education

Nearly all respondents (85%) foresaw the need for support from their organisations if they were to undertake alcohol education in the future. Those who did not indicated that they would seek support from other sources such as self-help groups and voluntary counsellors. Only a small proportion (29%) had started to negotiate this support before attending the DC course, although 42% indicated that someone else from their organisation had already initiated support. Health Education Units, Councils on Alcoholism and street level advice centres appear to be the focal points for such support.

The national data, therefore, support the conclusion of Debbie Clarke in Chapter 2 that clear pre-course information is vitally important. The concept of the key tutor is both misunderstood and misinterpreted with the result that many participants and their managers remain unaware of:

1. the expectation that the individual will commit a considerable amount of his/her work time to running further DC courses;

2. the expectation that the management will actively support this commitment by making resources, materials and work time available to the individual.

The list below gives some of the reasons why participants feel unable or unwilling to run full DC courses:

(a) Not enough time in my present job.

(b) I am not responsible for training.

(c) I came mainly for personal development.

(d) No backing or support from management.

(e) I can not arrange for other colleagues to be released to attend the course.

(f) I did not realise this was expected of me.

Sources of information on DC

The variety of sources of information on DC courses at national level echoes that found in the South West. There are both formal and informal channels of communication and the results highlight the need for training officers, Health Education Units and local Councils on Alcoholism to be supplied with clear, accurate information about the purpose of DC courses. There are one or two surprising responses to the question "How did you hear about the course?". One respondent said he had received an invitation from the National Council on Alcoholism (an organisation which ceased to operate over two years ago!) and another admitted 'liberating' an invitation from a colleague's in-tray! A small percentage of respondents (5%) thought that their courses had been organised as part of the HEC alcohol education programme in the South West. As none in this analysis had, this acts as a reminder to course organisers that workers outside the alcohol field are not necessarily 'au fait' with regional or national developments.

Participants: do they get what they want?

After attending a DC course, participants are asked to give general reflections on the 'feel' of their course. They comment on the workload, the stress level, the balance of occupations represented, the facilitators' performance and the degree of group identity developed by the course. The responses are as positive, if not more so, as those from the South West courses. Some 92% thought the course was never or only occasionally stressful, 87% defined the group spirit as excellent or very good and 80% rated the facilitators' performance as excellent or very good. Participants were not as happy with the balance of occupations represented, however, as 57% felt that there were either some relevant groups missing or that there were too many from one particular background. The latter can hardly be avoided in the case of single discipline courses and adds further weight to the argument for multidiscipinary courses. Respondents felt that, in particular, the fields of social work, probation, teaching and medicine were under-represented and that it was preferable to work in mixed discipline groups for the different perspectives they provided.

Before coming on a course, participants are asked to select three main things they hope to gain from the experience. Results from the national data indicate a more diffuse range of needs and expectations than that seen in the South West. In common with the South West, the most pressing needs expressed by participants related to the acquisition of knowledge, and to confidence in applying participative learning techniques to alcohol education. Nearly a third of respondents, however, saw personal development as an extremely important issue. Many indicated that they were thinking beyond the immediate outcomes of the course by hoping to gain confidence in applying participative learning techniques to other topics and confidence to present alcohol education talks. Another popular expectation was that DC would provide participants with the confidence to use alcohol education as part of a client treatment programme. From the outset it is evident that participants hope that DC will in the main, add to and enhance their current level of involvement in alcohol education rather than equip them to act as key tutors. A mere 10% (as in the South West) expressed any interest in gaining confidence to run full DC courses. Instead, 26% of participants listed a desire for more information on alcohol related issues as what they most wanted out of the event. The post course questionnaire indicated that 48% of respondents felt that more information on alcohol related issues had been their main gain from the DC course.

Using the DC experience

The majority of DC participants stated that, as a result of the course, their ability to be an alcohol educator had improved (89%). No one felt that their ability had actually declined although 11% felt that they had remained static. Of this 11% several people already possessed considerable skills in alcohol education before attending the course.

The majority of participants (62%) felt that they would go on to use substantial parts of the DC course in the future, although only 13% felt ready to commit themselves to running a full course. There was a noticeable degree of uncertainty about these two courses of action in that 31% people did not know whether they would use part of DC and 27% did not know whether they would run a full course or not. People were asked to identify the main blockage they might encounter in applying the skills taught on DC courses to their everyday work and over half highlighted the lack of resources (ie time, literature, rooms, etc). The lack of time concerned almost everyone either because they felt their own workloads to be sufficiently heavy or because they felt their managers would be unwilling and unco-operative in making work time available. Other comments included:

1. lack of opportunity for alcohol education in my job;

2. the known difficulty of implementing health education;

3. I work on a 1:1 basis, not in groups;

4. the course is too liberal for me, it is pro-drinking.

Networks of support

As 89% of participants felt that DC had improved their skills in alcohol education and a total of 75% felt they would go on to use the whole course or parts of it in their daily work, the question of how to provide continued support arises. As Debbie Clarke points out in her chapter, information, skills and knowledge passed on in the 'cascade' model of training risk becoming depleted and the enthusiasm and impetus engendered by the course can drain away if participants are not given further stimulation and support. Many participants anticipate applying what they learn on DC to other health-related topics such as smoking, nutrition and drug education carried out with a variety of client groups such as pregnant women and elderly people. To ensure that these valid applications of DC principles and techniques are neither overlooked nor undervalued, the possibility of a follow-up or refresher session is discussed on the final day of the course and arrangements left in the hands of the course convenor and one or two volunteer participants.

In addition to Questionnaire III, which will be circulated to participants, the Addictions Project also asks each course convenor to complete a questionnaire to assess whether follow-up sessions have been held and whether networks of support have been established. Although only a small number of replies have been received to date, it appears that most DC courses hold a follow-up session and that small, localised networks of support are slowly beginning to emerge. Participants are also asked what type of follow-up they would like. Their replies include:

1.   further training days;

2.   back up and resources from health education department;

3.   further contact with other group members;

4.   management support.

Many responses refer to 'latest techniques', 'more information' and 'updates' which seems to indicate that, although DC can significantly improve individuals' abilities in alcohol education, it does not do such a thorough job in increasing confidence to tackle alcohol education. Respondents seem to fear becoming out dated in terms of both knowledge and techniques although some recognise the value of further contact with each other and emphasise the importance of liaison and teamwork in organising future alcohol education activities.

Influence of DC on the new drugs/solvents package

As mentioned in the introduction to this chapter, the Addictions Project was also asked to develop a new training package on drugs and solvents which would be aimed at professionals who deal primarily with adults rather than children.[2]   The package, currently known by its working title 'Dealing with Drugs' (DWD), has been written in line with DC principles and incorporates many of the lessons learned from the national dissemination of the alcohol education course. These include:

Good points about DC	Not so good points about DC
Knowledge, attitudes, skills approach.	Occasionally veers from 'education' into 'treatment'.
Participatory learning techniques.	Pre-specified learning objectives can be restricting.
Practical exercises for use in alcohol education.	Could be more participant-centred.

Accordingly, DWD was based on the humanistic view of learning which says that:

1. participants should be self-directed learners;

2. the trainer's role is to facilitate rather than direct;

3. participants will bring experiences related to drugs to the course. These can be used as resources for learning, to which new learning will be related;

4. participants will help each other to learn by sharing experiences;

5. participants will identify their own learning needs and set their own goals;

6. facilitators will encourage participants to evaluate their own learning as they go through the course;

7. learning will be experiential;

8. learning will be centred on the immediate needs and problems of the learners;

9. the facilitator will endeavour to create a safe, trusting environment.

Change of model

It was felt, following a review of models available for drug education, that the traditional <u>objectives model</u> of curriculum development was not appropriate for the 'Dealing with Drugs' course for several reasons. Firstly, this model takes a mechanistic, behavioural view of people, which is in direct conflict with the humanistic model on which the course was to be based. It presumes that learning objectives can be set at the outset, implying that learners are passive recipients of teacher-specified goals. This view was contrary to the basic philosophy of DWD, that facilitators and participants were partners in learning and that learning experiences should be student-centred.

There were other more practical objections to specifying behavioural objectives in detail. The DWD writers felt unable to anticipate, in detail, all the relevant learning which could take place on a course based on experiential, participative exercises. Much of what we commonly understand as 'learning', does not show up as easily measurable, observable behaviour. The writers anticipated that many controversial, emotive issues would be raised by the package and that to pre-specify learning objectives on such occasions would almost amount to indoctrination. The proposed course would not lend itself to evaluation carried out by traditional formal, written or oral examination of participants and it was felt that precise behavioural objectives such as "participants will be able to state three types of depressant drugs" were inappropriate.

Accordingly, DWD was planned using an alternative model, the process model, which places emphasis on the basic principles which underpin the course, rather than on pre-specified objectives. The following key principles inform all the teaching and learning activities of the course:

1. to promote the principles and practice of effective drug education;

2. to promote interest and involvement in drug education;

3. to promote responsibility in drug use.

The training package concerns itself with drug education only and is not tempted to wander over into treatment or counselling issues. It aims to develop:

1. an up-to-date knowledge of the basic facts about drugs needed for drug education;

2. an appreciation that the use of drugs forms part of an overall continuum of human behaviour;

3. an understanding of how drugs are used responsibly and irresponsibly and the effects of irresponsible drug use on individuals, families and society;

4. a knowledge of the strengths and weaknesses of various approaches to drug education;

5. the confidence and competence of participants to act as drug educators.

The materials cover five days of training which are intended to be run in two blocks of three days and two days. This reflects the model on which DC is run at the national level. In the interim period on a DC course, participants are expected to undertake some action research on helping agencies. This practice has been amended slightly in DWD and participants are primed for and expected to undertake some drug education fieldwork during the interim period and report back on its strengths and weaknesses. Also, a half day session in DWD (morning of Day Five) has been left unstructured to allow participants to plan and design their own learning activities in relation to options which interest them particularly.

Extensive trials of the materials have been carried out and it is expected that the final version of the package will be published by the Health Education Council in June 1987. A national programme of dissemination will follow.

What of the future?

Several points made in the earlier chapters of this publication by Kevin Doogan and Debbie Clarke are borne out by lessons learned at the national level. The key tutor concept and the pyramid or 'cascade' model of training are both problematic and do not appear to fulfil their individual purpose. The following suggestions might, in each case, go some way towards improving the situation.

1. Key tutor concept

(a) Much stricter selection of participants to ensure that they have an explicit role in alcohol education.

(b) Involvement of participants' managers to ensure that DC's aims and objectives are understood and that future commitment to alcohol education (in terms of time, resources and active management support) is agreed on.

(c) Recommended pre-course reading to raise participants' awareness of key debates and perspectives in the alcohol field. This could inform all discussion and debate taking place on the course itself.

(d) Courses to concentrate more on developing training and communication skills for key tutors than on the content of the DC manual itself.

2. The pyramid 'cascade' model

Further to the points made above:

(a) Financial backing for regional networks of support for trained DC tutors.

(b) Regional appointees to utilise finances to provide refresher days, updates, skills workshops, newsletters and whatever else a region's tutors may decide they need in terms of support.

This revised model is very similar to that used with 'Look After Yourself!'[3] tutors which has enjoyed some success. It would seem that after good organisation, the crucial ingredient appears to be money. If all of these points were adopted, however, there would be a very real risk of elevating DC out of the market place. There would be so many criteria to satisfy before going on a course, that both would-be participants and eager tutors could be deterred! To aim for a key tutor course where 20 participants undertake training and then run 20 subsequent courses is to aim for an ideal which cannot possibly exist in reality.

There must surely be a place for multidisciplinary DC courses where participants share and increase their knowledge, clarify their attitudes and enhance their skills in alcohol education without committing themselves to running full courses. Most DC courses at national level are run on this basis, in the full knowledge that the majority of participants come on a DC course for personal benefits which they plough back into their everyday work by means of an increased knowledge and ability to use new skills and techniques. This may invalidate the key tutor concept but in no way undermines the aims and objectives set out in the DC manual. Both the course content and the participatory learning approach are frequently praised and appreciated by participants who feel motivated to select parts of the course, methods of presentation and some of the techniques for future use. This adaptation of DC materials to individual work situations should be neither overlooked nor undervalued. The national DC programme also introduces participants to the manual gradually and allows time for discussion of what happens after the course and what support and follow-up course members feel they need.

Conclusion

It is inevitable that no single package of training materials or model of dissemination can hope to meet all training needs, but it is important to learn from and build on experiences to date. The new 'Dealing with Drugs' package incorporates a more student-centred approach and aims to develop individuals' skills in planning and presenting educational in-puts. As recommended by Kevin Doogan, there is time built into the drugs pack to allow for "training in negotiation skills, the sharing of experiences in overcoming institutional obstacles and developing good practice in establishing support networks etc".[4] The proposed dissemination model also differs slightly from that used with DC. Participants with a proven role in drug education (such as health education/promotion staff) will train in pairs on a regional dissemination course. They will return to their districts and support each other in further drug education activities tailored to meet district needs. It is anticipated that regional networks of support will develop to maintain enthusiasm and to allow examples of good practice to be shared.

Finally, it is likely that a study of the two methods of dissemination (ie the DC model and the DWD model) and their individual outcomes will be made.

References

1. Simnett, I., Wright, L. and Evans, M. (1982) Drinking choices: a training manual for alcohol educators, TACADE/HEC.

2. The Health Education Council have previously funded the Teachers' Advisory Council for Alcohol and Drug Education to develop and disseminate training packages for professionals who work with children and young people.

3. Look After Yourself courses have been developed by the Health Education Council and provided through local tutors who often work within the adult education provision of local authorities.

4. **Doogan, K.** Chapter 3, p 50.

6

CONCLUSION: THEMES AND ISSUES

Robin Means and Lyn Harrison

Introduction

This brief final chapter will reflect on four important themes and issues that flow out of the five previous chapters. Before this is attempted, however, it is necessary to remind readers of the preliminary nature of the research that has so far been carried out on 'Drinking Choices' courses both in the South West and at a national level. Many questions remain unanswered about the long term alcohol education activity of those who have been trained and this will be a theme of future publications.

However, the initial research confirmed the limitations of the 'cascade' model and led into an important dialogue with certain key trainers such as Barbara Howe and Derek Close. It seemed important to offer the fruits of this dialogue to a wider audience because of its implications for those who are trying to develop training strategies in alcohol and drug education at a more local level.

Learning from evaluative research

The most striking point raised by Chapter 1 was the failure to take on board enough of the lessons from the Brandes[1] research on the Tyne Tees experience. Her PhD clearly illustrates the limitations of the 'cascade' model, which, as Clarke points out in Chapter 2, "is often better in theory than in practice". Brandes indicated that most participants lacked the confidence to run their own full courses or they were not in an organisational position to do so. She offered a series of recommendations that might reduce these obstacles.

A process of re-learning this lesson has occurred at a South West and national level as indicated by Chapters 4 and 5. The emerging training strategy of the South West alcohol education programme and the new 'Dealing with Drugs' pack seems to take an increasingly realistic view of what can and what cannot be achieved through the use of 'cascade' principles.

There is nothing unusual about the failure of the previous research to influence future policy. Numerous commentators such as Randall Smith,[2] Gilbert Smith[3] and Pat Thomas[4] have discussed this failure over a very wide range of policy areas, from social work practice to policies for the inner city. Research takes a long time and often produces results 'too late' for the real world, is often presented in a format that is difficult to assimilate and recommendations often fail to reflect the practical constraints on the policy maker. As Howe points out, it would be easy to develop a selection process for DC course entry and mechanisms of post course support that were totally unrealistic. The need to make research findings accessible in terms of cost, language and location is one we would like to stress. Findings do not have to be presented only as a final academic report to the funders, but can take a variety of forms such as workshops, short summary reports or an ongoing dialogue between researchers, funders and the policy world.

This publication has illustrated how such a dialogue has occurred between the SAUS evaluation team and the staff of the South West alcohol education programme. Initial fears about the 'failure' of the 'cascade' model in the dissemination programme were confirmed by the research and appropriate adjustments made. However, evidence from the postal questionnaires also emphasised the level of alcohol education activity of key tutor course participants, even if most had not gone on to run their own full courses. These efforts are listed in the Appendix to Doogan's chapter. When asked to list their alcohol education activities in the six months after the course, 11 of the 46 respondents were unable to give any examples. This group included three health education officers, all of whom have, nevertheless, been active in the South West programme. All three have helped to organise briefing conferences and all three have been successful in making a case to their district health authority for a local co-ordinator post. It would appear they have used their increased knowledge about alcohol education issues to good effect even if they lacked the time to run specific training events for other professionals. The other 35 respondents show a wide spread of activities from the counselling of four individual clients by a social worker to the running of four full courses that have trained 62 people by a voluntary sector manager. To remind the reader of five other examples:

1. DCM used as preparation for the commencement of an alcohol education programme run jointly by the Council on Alcoholism and the Probation Service. Each course contains eight consecutive sessions of two hours each (probation officer).

2. A stimulus to a wide range of activities including setting up briefing conferences, forming local alcohol forums, study days and workshops. With regard to the last two, she had helped to run a weekend course for youth leaders and a presentation to the Safety Committee of a local district council (health education officer).

3. This individual has run two different one day workshops in conjunction with a fellow key tutor. She has used material and approach of DCM in her health education work in secondary schools. This involves 400 pupils in groups of 17-24 (school teacher/head teacher).

4. Organised evening session of youth club (community youth worker).

5. This tutor has been involved in development of a scheme to raise interest and awareness in the hospital. This has included the introduction of alcohol education as a specific part of the new nurse training curriculum (nurse/nurse tutor).

These research findings, together with the resultant changes in the training strategy of the South West programme, led the evaluation team to re-assess the initial focus of the postal questionnaires upon whether participants were going on to run their own full courses. Instead, it seemed more important to clarify the subsequent volume and variety of alcohol education training activity of key tutor course participants. Therefore, the questionnaires now ask participants to list each of their training activities over the last six months under the most appropriate heading of the six listed below:

(a) 'one-off' talk or presentation;

(b) 'one-off' day workshop on alcohol education;

(c) training programme on alcohol education for professionals (residential or series of sessions);

(d) training programme on alcohol education for clients, patients, school pupils, parents or other consumers (residential or series of sessions);

(e)   training programme which applies participatory learning techniques to other health topics;

(f)   other (please specify).

This may provide a fairer and more realistic mechanism to judge the impact of key tutor courses upon participants.

Training the trainers

Bolam and Medlock[5] carried out an evaluation of a series of training courses for teachers and social education advisers that was designed to disseminate the importance of Active Tutorial Work[6] in schools. Bolam and Medlock explain that active tutorial work is designed to equip young people with those personal and social skills which are the foundation of self esteem and personal health. It represents "a breakthrough" since teachers are being asked to "use active, experiential learning in real life settings".[7]   National dissemination had been handled through a series of courses run by Jill Baldwin and Andy Smith and there has been a growing demand for such events from LEAs and teachers. However, Bolam and Medlock note how "an unavoidable consequence of the charismatic appeal of the National Directors is that other training leaders find it difficult to match their performance".[8]

This is also an issue with regard to the Drinking Choices Manual. There is a danger that participants will feel inhibited by the level of facilitator skills exhibited by a national or regional trainer. In this respect, moves in the South West to develop training teams around local co-ordinators may be very important, as will the use of workshops to further develop training skills. The test of such training manuals then, ceases to be the full implementation of a 'cascade' model but rather whether each district or local authority is developing its own training capacity. This, also, implies that national and regional disseminators should be encouraged to run less courses and, instead, spend more time acting as consultants to existing local trainers. This needs to be combined with a greater emphasis on clearer targeting and the development of local training strategies.

Clarke raised the issue of the dilution of the experiential approach after the initial course input. In other words, participants remember the factual information on alcohol but they increasingly fail to use it in participative settings. This further underlines the need to ensure that districts, regions and local authorities contain individuals with facilitator skills who are committed to the development of alcohol and drug education.

Targeting

The Drinking Choices Manual stresses that "all of us at one time or another are alcohol educators" and gives 38 examples of "some groups who could act as alcohol educators".[9] This was not seen as problematic since a commitment to inter-disciplinary working was part of the central ethos of the training package.

Several of the chapters listed the gains from this. Both Doogan and Howe indicate that the consequent sharing of perspectives in alcohol education is a central reason why these courses are so valued by most participants.

However, both Clarke and Close raised the issue of the need for more focused targeting for particular courses. Both were aware of the tension that arises when half a group wish to concentrate upon their group work skills and the other half want to concentrate upon increasing their alcohol education knowledge. This tension between those who are process led and those who are content led was, also, found by Bolam and Medlock[10] in their research on Active Tutorial Work dissemination courses. The previous section does suggest that the careful targeting of local trainers may be crucial to the development of a long-term impetus to alcohol education training.

Clarke, also, argued for single department courses on the grounds that this facilitates the development of future training plans. Howe, on the other hand, indicated that her own experience of such courses confirmed her belief in the need for a multi-disciplinary perspective. A compromise between these two positions is to attempt to clarify what professionals are likely to be 'working together' on a day-to-day basis. All participants may enjoy a multi-disciplinary course but a road safety officer is unlikely to have regular dealings with a social worker. Professionals apply alcohol education in the context of their organisational worlds. Previous research by Pearson et al[11] on professional responses to heroin users and by Blaxter et al[12] on alcohol abuse in the Western Isles have both underlined that statutory agencies address substance abuse from the perspective of their statutory responsibilities and roles. A commitment to inter-disciplinary work does not mean that differences between professional groups can be ignored. Why do probation officers tend to talk about alcohol and crime? Why do social workers talk about alcohol and child abuse? Why do teachers talk about alcohol and young people? The answer is obviously that organisational role and professional training influence perceptions of the potential focus for alcohol education. Such views can be challenged - but they do need to be understood. This situation perhaps implies that more courses should target particular types of professional rather than being as all embracing as sometimes occurs at the moment.

Whichever individuals/organisations and professionals are targeted for particular courses a process of 'selecting out' should be allowed for both at the beginning and end of the course. This could be based on information received through a pre-course meeting and literature made available at the beginning of the course. At the end of the course, provided it had been true to its own philosophy, individuals with different perspectives on alcohol problems and how to approach them would feel comfortable in acknowledging that they did not wish to engage actively in this form of alcohol education. The need to ensure a mutual respect between individuals and agencies working within the alcohol field is an important prerequisite for success in an activity such as the South West alcohol education programme.

The need for training strategies

The central message of this publication for the editors is that training packages such as the Drinking Choices Manual[13] are an invaluable mechanism for developing the training skills of individuals but that this needs to be combined with a greater awareness from health authorities and local authorities that the consequent enthusiasm needs to be integrated within local training strategies.

This does create something of a 'chicken and egg' problem. The participants will have limited effectiveness without such strategies. The development of such strategies at a local level may require a heavy 'push' from former participants. Certainly Tether and Robinson in Preventing alcohol problems: a guide to local action[14] have underlined the enormous scope for local intervention within existing legislation. The crucial question is whether such intervention will remain dependent upon the energy and enthusiasm of a few individuals or whether it will be systematically incorporated into organisational practice so that its continuance ceases to be dependent on the original innovator. In the context of training, this means that alcohol education should be coherently developed within professional and in-service training programmes rather than just the province of imaginative one-off events. Organisations will have to be shifted as well as individuals.

This was a message which came out clearly from the chapters by Doogan, Howe and Close. It is not sufficient to select individuals carefully for the programme, since even those already with an active training role are not necessarily able to incorporate or develop an alcohol education strategy into their organisation. Organisations must be willing to give more support and resources to the course participant than just the time needed to attend.

A process of negotiation is needed at both the individual and organisational level which must occur before the beginning of the course and should continue after it. This, along with an acknowledgment of organisational problems as a course component, could well enhance the future effectiveness of course participants and the dissemination of sensible drinking practices into a variety of organisational settings.

References

1. **Brandes, D.** (1985) An illuminative evaluation of an alcohol education project, PhD Thesis, University of Durham.

2. **Smith, R.C.** (1981) 'Implementing the results of evaluation studies' in **Barrett, S. and Fudge, C.** (eds) Policy and Action, London: Methuen.

3. **Smith, G.** (1983) 'Social work, policy, government and research: a mildly optimistic view' in **Gardy, J., et al,** (eds) Improving social intervention, London: Croom Helm.

4. **Thomas, P.** (1985) The aims and outcomes of social policy research, London: Croom Helm.

5. **Bolam, R., and Medlock, P.** (1985) Active tutorial work: training and dissemination - an evaluation, Oxford: Blackwell.

6. The actual teaching materials are laid out in a series of publications, see **Baldwin, J. and Wells, H.** (eds) (1979-1983), Active tutorial work, Books 1-5 and 16-19, Oxford: Blackwell.

7. **Bolam and Medlock,** op cit, p 3.

8. **Ibid,** p 61.

9. **Simnett, I., Wright, L. and Evans, M.** (1982) <u>Drinking choices:</u>
    <u>a training manual for alcohol educators</u>, TACADE/HEC, p 7.

10. **Bolam and Medlock,** op cit, pp 49-55.

11. **Pearson, G., Gilman, M. and McIver, S.** (1985) <u>Young people</u>
    <u>and heroin</u>, London: HEC, Research Report No 8.

12. **Blaxter, M., Mullen, K. and Dyer, S.** (1982) <u>Problems of</u>
    <u>alcohol abuse in the Western Isles: a community study</u>,
    Scottish Home and Health Department, Scottish Health
    Service Studies No 44.

13. **Simnett et al,** op cit.

14. **Tether, P. and Robinson, D.** (1986) <u>Preventing alcohol</u>
    <u>problems: a guide to local action</u>, London: Tavistock.

APPENDIX

HEALTH EDUCATION COUNCIL'S 'DRINKING CHOICES' COURSES

QUESTIONNAIRE I

This questionnaire is to be completed immediately <u>before</u> attending a 'Drinking Choices' course.

PERSONAL DETAILS

1. Name

    ....

2. Please state the name and address of your organisation.
    (If you are <u>not</u> in relevant paid employment, please answer this question in respect of your voluntary activity.)

    (a) Name ....

    (b) Address ....

         ....

         ....

         ....

3. Please state below your post within the organisation listed above.

    ....

    ....

    ....

4. Please tick the <u>one</u> box which best describes the
   post you have stated in Question 3.

   (i)   Community worker, youth worker

   (ii)   General practitioner

   (iii)   Health education officer

   (iv)   Health visitor

   (v)   Hospital doctor

   (vi)   Nurse/nurse tutor

   (vii)   Personnel/welfare officer

   (viii) Police officer

   (ix)   Probation

   (x)   School teacher/head teacher

   (xi)   Social worker/manager/trainer

   (xii)   Voluntary counsellor

   (xiii) Self-employed

   (xiv) Voluntary sector manager

   (xv)   Other

            If other, please specify below

            ....

5. Does your job include a major training responsibility?
   (If you are <u>not</u> in relevant paid employment, please
   answer this question in respect of your voluntary
   activity.)

                     Yes

                     No

THE 'DRINKING CHOICES' COURSE

6. Please state how you heard about the 'Drinking Choices' course

   ....

   ....

7. Is the 'Drinking Choices' course organised through the HEC alcohol education programme in the South West?

   <u>Tick</u>

   Yes
   No

8. Please indicate in order of preference (ie mark 1st, 2nd, 3rd) <u>a maximum</u> of <u>three</u> things you want out of the 'Drinking Choices' course.

   (i)   More information on alcohol related issues.

   (ii)   Confidence to apply participative learning techniques to alcohol education.

   (iii)   Confidence to apply participative learning techniques to other health related topics.

   (iv)   Confidence to run a full 'Drinking Choices' course.

   (v)   Confidence to use alcohol education as part of a client treatment programme.

   (vi)   Confidence to present alcohol education talks.

   (vii)   An opportunity to meet other people in the field.

   (viii) Personal development.

   (ix)   Other

           If other, please specify below

   ....

9.   Would any future alcohol education activities by you
     rely on substantial support from within your organisation?

                                                              <u>Tick</u>

                                            Yes
                                            No

     If you have answered no, please explain why you will
     be able to proceed without support.

     ....

     ....

10. If you have answered yes to Question 9

     (i)   Have you started to negotiate this support?

                                                              <u>Tick</u>

                                            Yes
                                            No

     (ii)   If yes, with whom?
            (Please state the job or role of the individual(s)
            and <u>not</u> their name(s).)

            ....

            ....

     (iii) Has someone from your organisation already
            initiated this support?

                                                              <u>Tick</u>

                                            Yes
                                            No

     (iv)   If yes, who?
            (Please state the job or role of the individual(s)
            and <u>not</u> their name(s).)

            ....

            ....

FEELINGS ABOUT ALCOHOL EDUCATION

11.   Who do you think can benefit <u>most</u> from alcohol
        education?

                                                        <u>Tick</u>

        People with severe drinking problems
        Most people who drink
        Do not know

12.   Do you believe that alcohol education can change
        the drinking patterns of the general population?

                                                        <u>Tick</u>

                                    Yes
                                    Not
                                    sure
                                    No

13.   How confident do you feel about your ability to be
        an alcohol educator?

                                                        <u>Tick</u>

                            Very confident
                            Fairly confident
                            Do not know
                            Unconfident

HEALTH EDUCATION COUNCIL'S 'DRINKING CHOICES' COURSES

QUESTIONNAIRE II

This questionnaire is to be completed immediately <u>after</u> attending a 'Drinking Choices' course.

1.   Name

....

EXPERIENCE OF THE 'DRINKING CHOICES' COURSE

2.   Did you find the workload during the course

<u>Tick</u>

Too full
Just about right
Not full enough

3.   How stressful did you find the course?

<u>Tick</u>

Often stressful
Occasionally stressful
Never stressful

4.   Consider the people present on the course and their organisational and professional backgrounds: to what extent do you think the balance of backgrounds was correct?

<u>Tick</u>

Too many from one particular background
Some relevant groups missing
Just about right

4. If you would like to commment more on your answer please do so below.

....

....

5. Please rate the course you have just attended for each of the following

   (i)   Group spirit/identity

<u>Tick</u>

                Excellent
                Very good
                Good
                Moderate
                Fair

   (ii)   Performance of leader(s)

<u>Tick</u>

                Excellent
                Very good
                Good
                Moderate
                Fair

   (iii) Scope of information in the manual

<u>Tick</u>

                Excellent
                Very good
                Good
                Moderate
                Fair

   (iv) Presentation of the material from the manual

<u>Tick</u>

                Excellent
                Very good
                Good
                Moderate
                Fair

6. If you would like to pass any other comments on the course please do so below.

    ....

    ....

    ....

EFFECTIVENESS OF THE 'DRINKING CHOICES' COURSE

7. As a result of the course do you feel your ability to be an alcohol educator has

                                                        Tick

                        Improved
                        Stayed the same
                        Declined

8. Who do you think can benefit <u>most</u> from alcohol education?

                                                        Tick

            People with severe drinking problems
            Most people who drink
            Do not know

9. Do you believe that alcohol education can change the drinking patterns of the general population?

                                                        Tick

                        Yes
                        Not sure
                        No

10. Please indicate below in order of preference (ie mark 1st, 2nd, 3rd) a <u>maximum</u> of <u>three</u> things which you feel you have gained from the course.

(i) More information on alcohol related issues.

(ii) Confidence to apply participative learning techniques to alcohol education.

(iii) Confidence to apply participative learning techniques to other health related topics.

(iv) Confidence to run a full 'Drinking Choices' course.

(v) Confidence to use alcohol education as part of a client treatment programme.

(vi) Confidence to present alcohol education talks.

(vii) An opportunity to meet other people in the field.

(viii) Personal development.

(ix) Other

If other, please specify below

....

11. Please specify the <u>main</u> blockage you may encounter in applying the skills taught on the 'Drinking Choices' course in your everyday work (tick <u>one</u> box only).

    (i)   Lack of confidence.

    (ii)   Lack of resources (eg time, literature, rooms, etc).

    (iii) Alcohol education is not perceived as an appropriate activity for your organisation.

    (iv)   Disagree personally with much of the content of the 'Drinking Choices' course.

    (v)   Other.

           If other, please specify below

           ....

12. To what extent do you feel the 'Drinking Choices' course supported the following statements

    (i)   Alcohol education is everyone's business

                                                            <u>Tick</u>

                            Strongly
                            Moderately
                            Not at all
                            Do not know

    (ii)   Alcohol education should be based on a participatory learning model

                                                            <u>Tick</u>

                            Strongly
                            Moderately
                            Not at all
                            Do not know

(iii)   Alcohol education should aim to enable everyone
to make informed choices about the use of alcohol

<u>Tick</u>

Strongly
Moderately
Not at all
Do not know

13.   To what extent do you personally support the
following statements:

(i)   Alcohol education is everyone's business

<u>Tick</u>

Strongly
Moderately
Not at all
Do not know

(ii)   Alcohol education should be based on a participatory
learning model

<u>Tick</u>

Strongly
Moderately
Not at all
Do not know

(iii)   Alcohol education should aim to enable everyone
to make informed choices about the use of alcohol

<u>Tick</u>

Strongly
Moderately
Not at all
Do not know

101

14. Do you expect to use substantial <u>parts</u> of the 'Drinking Choices' course with groups in the near future?

<u>Tick</u>

Yes
No
Do not know

15. Do you expect to run a <u>full</u> 'Drinking Choices' course in the near future?

<u>Tick</u>

Yes
No
Do not know

16. What 'follow-up' support do you feel you need in addition to that likely to be available from your organisation, to help you function as an alcohol educator?

....
....
....
....
....
....

HEALTH EDUCATION COUNCIL'S 'DRINKING CHOICES' COURSES

QUESTIONNAIRE III

This questionnaire is being used twice a year to follow up the activities of all participants from the 'Drinking Choices' courses.

1.   Name

....

2.   Please indicate below in order of preference (ie mark 1st, 2nd, 3rd) a <u>maximum</u> of <u>three</u> things from the 'Drinking Choices' course you attended which have proved to be useful in your everyday work.

    (i)   More information on alcohol related issues.

    (ii)   Confidence to apply participative learning techniques to alcohol education.

    (iii)   Confidence to apply participative learning techniques to other health related topics.

    (iv)   Confidence to run a full 'Drinking Choices' course.

    (v)   Confidence to use alcohol education as part of a client treatment programme.

    (vi)   Confidence to present alcohol education talks.

    (vii) An opportunity to meet other people in the field.

    (viii) Personal development.

    (ix)   Other

          If other, please specify below

          ....

3. Did you intend to run a <u>full</u> 'Drinking Choices' course after you had attended a course yourself?

Tick

Yes
No

4. (a) Have you run a <u>full</u> 'Drinking Choices' course yourself?

Tick

Yes
No

    (b) If yes, please indicate the date, location and number of participants for the course.

<u>Date</u>	<u>Location</u>	<u>Course leader(s)</u>	<u>Number of Participants</u>

    (c) Please attach a list of the participants' names, addresses and employment (paid or voluntary) if possible.

5. If you have not run a full 'Drinking Choices' course, on reflection to what extent was this due to? (Please tick one box only.)

(i) Lack of confidence.

(ii) Lack of resources (eg time, literature, rooms, etc).

(iii) Alcohol education is not perceived as an appropriate activity for your organisation.

(iv) Disagree personally with much of the content of the 'Drinking Choices' course.

(v) Other.

If other, please specify below

....

6. Has a 'Drinking Choices' support network developed locally?

Tick

Yes
No
Do not know

7. If you have answered yes to Question 6, please describe the nature of this network.

....
....
....
....

8. Please list <u>any</u> alcohol education activities which you have organised as a result of you attending the 'Drinking Choices' course.

....

....

....

....

9. If you have any other comments you would like to make about your alcohol education activities since attending the 'Drinking Choices' course please specify below.

....

....

....

....

RECENT PUBLICATIONS FROM SAUS

OCCASIONAL PAPERS

OP 21 Pub drinking and the licensed trade: a study of
drinking cultures and local community in two
areas of South West England
Adrian Franklin (1985)   £4.30

OP 22 Implementing an inner city policy: a review of
the London Borough of Hammersmith and Fulham
Inner Area Programme
Gill Whitting (1985)   £5.45

OP 23 Shutting out the inner city worker: recruitment
and training practices of large employers in
central London
Tom Davies and Charlie Mason (1986)   £4.30

OP 24 Milton Keynes - the best of both worlds? Public
and professional views of a new city
Jeff Bishop (September 1986)   £6.55

OP 25 Educating about alcohol: professional
perspectives and practice in South West England
Robin Means, Lyn Harrison, Lesley Hoyes and
Randall Smith (1986)   £6.55

OP 26 Building societies: the way forward
Derek Hawes (August 1986)   £4.75

OP 27 Centralisation and decentralisation in England
and France
Stephen Garrish (September 1986)   £6.55

OP 28 Decentralisation and democracy: localising
public services
Edited by Paul Hoggett and Robin Hambleton
(March 1987)   £6.95

SAUS STUDIES

SS 1 An unreasonable act? Central-local government
conflict and the Housing Act 1980
Ray Forrest and Alan Murie (1985)   £6.55

SS 2 Rethinking policy planning: a study of planning
       systems linking central and local government
       Robin Hambleton (September 1986)   £7.65

SS 3 Managing health services: health authority
       members in search of a role
       Chris Ham (November 1986)   £7.15

WORKING PAPERS

WP 60 Homelessness in London
       John Greve and others (1986)   £2.20

WP 61 The provision of counselling in an informal
       service for young people
       Frances Blackwell, John Habershon, Gill
       Whitting and Elizabeth Winter (1986)   £3.25

WP 62 Owner occupation, privatism and ontological
       security: a critical reformulation
       Adrian Franklin (1986)   £2.75

WP 63 Child abuse parents speaking: parents'
       impressions of social workers, and the social
       work process
       Celia Brown (1987)   £3.75

WP 64 Less complex and more stable: making block
       grant simpler
       Glen Bramley (1987)   £3.75

WP 65 Future of housing education: a symposium
       David Garnett (Spring 1987)   £3.00

WP 66 The national politics of alcohol education:
       a review
       Randall Smith (1987)   £3.85

All prices include postage. Please make cheques payable to the
University of Bristol.

For a full list of SAUS publications contact:

The Publications Officer, School for Advanced Urban Studies,
Rodney Lodge, Grange Road, BRISTOL BS8 4EA.
Telephone: (0272) 741117